I Believe ...

A Unique Collection of Truth, Wisdom and Common Sense

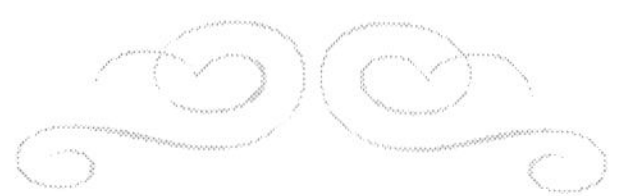

DANIEL TADDEO

PUBLISHED BY FIDELI PUBLISHING INC.

ISBN: 978-1-60414-744-5

CONTENTS

INTRODUCTION

Belief. What is it? It is one's acceptance, opinion, or conviction that a statement is true or real. It is also what guides how we choose to live every day.

I Believe... is just that, and what I believe can be traced back to the Bible's teachings, directly or indirectly. Over the years a person's beliefs can change, either through education or experience, but I have found the Bible to be a rock of truth upon which I, personally, find no error or contradictions. It is where I find direction and consolation, and what I do not understand completely, I take on faith.

At first I thought listing some of my beliefs would be easy and go quickly. I was amazed that once I focused on listening and experiencing each day with keen observation, I found a seemingly limitless amount to put down on paper. They are, however, only some of many, as every day I find more to ponder; they also are subject to change.

Whatever you believe, and no matter if you agree or disagree, it is my hope you find this book to be a source of reflection, inspiration, and perhaps learning. I also hope you find the statements on these pages to be uplifting, as I have. Perhaps they will cause you to question, confirm, or want to start your own list of beliefs.

— Daniel Taddeo

AMERICA

About half of Americans believe that an ongoing trend of people turning their backs on religion is bad for the country according to a recent Pew poll.

America does not have a revenue problem; it has a spending problem.

America is experiencing an awful scourge of moral decay among our children and young people because their parents and grandparents have largely "forgotten the laws of God."

American politics would be elevated by a renewed commitment to the common good.

Honorable citizens in America are on the decline from bottom to top.

One of the reasons America prospered was a strong emphasis on traditional family values that included instruction on the differences between right and wrong, teaching that began in the home and continued at school. One of the central sources for defining values was the Bible, which back then was found in all public schools.

The founders of America never intended to exclude God from the classroom because they knew that you had to have something proven upon which to base a system of values.

ATTITUDE

A cloudy day is no match for a sunny disposition.

A positive approach succeeds more than any other approach.

A word of encouragement to a hurting friend can come like a refreshing rain.

An attitude of gratitude benefits everyone.

Anyone in need is our neighbor.

Appreciate and enjoy today rather than dwell on yesterday and tomorrow.

Attitude keeps circumstances in proper perspective.

Attitudes are more important than facts.

Because time goes by so fast is all the more reason to enjoy the present moment.

Becoming more optimistic takes time, effort, and determination; but it can be done.

Correction does much; encouragement does more.

Courage, persistence, and perseverance guarantee positive results.

Discipline is absolutely necessary and it is a positive thing.

Do and say things that benefit all, whenever possible.

Every person is guilty of all the good he or she did not do.

Everybody is somebody in God's eyes.

Everyone should catch others doing right and praise them.

Everyone should socialize, optimize and exercise.

Everything we really need, we already have.

Fall seven times, stand up eight.

Generally, we praise only to be praised.

Giving of our time, talent and treasure is a good way to go.

I am only one, but I am one. I cannot do everything, but I can do something. What I can do, I should do, and with the help of God, I will do.

If we cannot say something positive, silence is the next best alternative.

If we exercise control over what we think, it is possible to control our attitudes and actions.

If you want to lift yourself up, lift up someone else.

It benefits everyone to delight in the success of others.

It is good to listen more and speak less.

It is more important to congratulate your partner when things go right than to console when things go wrong.

It is much more constructive to focus on what we have than not have.

It is our attitude and not our aptitude that determines our altitude.

Kindness matters most with most people. No matter how small, it is never wasted.

Many people in our society live by "it's all about me" attitude.

May we mend our ways, encourage one another, agree to disagree with one another, and live in peace.

No one can make you feel inferior without your consent.

No one is in charge of our happiness except us.

Optimism doesn't wait on facts. It relies on prospects.

Our words have the power to build up or tear down.

People should do whatever they can to help make the world a better place.

Praise and encouragement bring out the best in people and lift them up.

Sandwich every bit of criticism between two layers of praise.

Sincerity is the highest compliment one can pay.

Sometimes people just want us to be there, listen and understand.

Speak only good about people, not bad.

Strive every day to be a better person.

The greatest discovery of any generation is that human beings can alter their lives by altering their attitude.

Things turn out best for the people who make the most of the way things turn out.

Until we feel good about ourselves, it is almost impossible to encourage others.

We all experience sorrow, but we stand certain in the promises of God.

We are all subject to depression given the right set of circumstances; however there is a way out. It is by having a reason for living, a goal—one that can never be totally fulfilled in this lifetime because it is a growing and changing experience.

We are not stuck with our attitudes. We learned them. We can "unlearn" them.

We need to discover and express each other's positive aspects.

We need to encourage one another in times of despair and rely on faith, hope, and love.

We will gradually adopt the habits, attitudes, and mannerisms of the people with whom we spend a lot of time.

When we speak, our words should center on "that which is good to edify" and lift people up.

When we speak, our words should center on building others up.

Who we believe we are is what will play out in the long run.

You don't have to make yourself wrong to deliver an apology.

BEAUTY

Beauty in our culture is in major transition. It is moving from an internal, invisible beauty, such as heart-felt concern, mannerly conduct, and spirituality directed, to a physical, visible, and external beauty, such as extreme body decorations, indiscreet dress, and arrogant presentation. This "beauty-battle" rages between self-centeredness and God-centeredness.

Beauty, or lack thereof, is in the eye of the beholder.

Charm is deceptive and beauty is fleeting, but a woman who fears the Lord is to be praised.

It is a problem for youth when the goal of wellness turns into an obsession with them. We no longer honor the wisdom and beauty that can grow with age. We live in a death-denying culture.

It is better to be first with an "ugly" woman than the hundredth with a beauty.

Your beauty should not come from outward adornment, such as braided hair and the wearing of gold jewelry and fine clothes (acceptable in good taste but not required); instead, it should be that of your *inner self,* the unfading beauty of a gentle and quiet spirit, which is of great worth in God's sight.

BEHAVIOR

Act the way you want to be and soon you will be the way you act.

All of our thoughts can be divided into two basic categories: right and wrong. Right thoughts are God-centered and wrong thoughts are self-centered.

Always be yourself, because the people that matter don't mind, and the ones who mind don't matter.

Any new behavior feels a bit unnatural until we grow accustomed to it.

Anything founded on injustice never lasts.

At times our behavior will be appreciated, and at other times it will not. Our call is to trust God's word, not society's acceptance or rejection.

Attitude dictates our behavior.

Blaming prevents us from correcting the problem.

Complaints from people tell us what is in their hearts.

Despite one's own best efforts, things can and do go wrong.

Discover each other's positive traits of goodness, friendship, and love.

Do a good deed every day if you can; peace and joy will come if we accept God's plan.

Do not follow the crowd in doing wrong.

Doing something "just this once," knowing it is wrong, can lead to terrible consequences.

Don't argue with a know-it-all; he will drag you down to his level.

Effective listening is an important part of communicating.

Everyone's behavior impacts other people in a positive or negative way.

Exaggeration tends to weaken whatever we exaggerate.

Foolish people express their own opinions instead of trying to understand what others have to say.

Forgetting of a wrong is a mild revenge.

Forgive everyone everything.

Freedom is not a license to be non-law-abiding.

Get rid of anything that is not useful, beautiful or joyful.

Getting a collective community to take care of each other is the smart and right thing to do.

Good character is what we look for in others, and this is what others look for in us.

Good habits are hard to acquire but easy to live with. Bad habits are easy to acquire and hard to live with.

Honesty beats withholding the truth.

I must stand with anybody that stands right; stand with him while he is right and part with him when he goes wrong.

If we are going to make the most out of the rest of our lives, we cannot be stuck in the past.

If we spend our lives wishing (you name it), we may never enjoy (you name it).

If we think an unkind thought, we don't have to express it.

Improper conduct is the number one reason employees are fired and not promoted.

It is important to accept people where they are rather than where we expect them to be.

It is inborn for people to appeal to a standard of behavior, which they expect from others who also understand and follow.

It is possible, if we focus on it, to find fault with just about anything or everyone.

Let a man behave in his own house as a guest.

Let no one ever come to you without leaving better and happier.

Let our charity begin at home (our friends, coworkers and neighbors).

More people are making their own rules, setting their own standards, and living their own way. This can and in many ways will only end in disaster.

More people, male and female, young and old, are devoting more time to addictive pursuits, such as video games, the Internet, and sexual perversions.

Most of us do bad things. We betray friends, make hurtful remarks, and lie. We could reduce negative consequences if each one of us participated less.

Most of us tend to be better talkers than listeners.

Most people do what makes sense to them at the time.

Most people know what is right and what is wrong but choose to do otherwise.

Once we realize we do not have to be wrong to apologize, we will experience a new power.

One can be sincere and still be wrong.

One way to serve those in need is through day-to-day charitable giving.

Partial obedience is not considered obedience.

People do the best they can under the circumstances they find themselves.

People must accept the consequences of their bad behavior. Having it both ways is not an option.

Pleasing our peers can easily take us down the wrong road.

Reach out to everyone, even those who annoy you.

Saying only those things about people that you would say if they were present would contribute greatly to responsible conduct.

Shame is being aware of doing something wrong.

Sin is disobeying God's law. Deviant behavior is often no longer called sin; nevertheless, sin by any other name is still sin that produces negative consequences.

Some negative thoughts stand out more than others. The Really Awful Thoughts (RATs), such as those that dwell on our weaknesses, mistakes, and faults, can be more destructive than others.

Sticks and stones can break my bones and names can also hurt me.

The way to break a bad habit is to drop it!

There is nothing wrong with people possessing riches. The wrong surfaces when riches possess people.

Those who choose wickedness crave the darkness to hide their deeds.

Those who take responsibility for their actions set a good example.

Those who travel the "road of life" best are those who make the road better for those who follow.

To be wronged is an unending problem if we continue to remember it.

We are all slaves to sin (ungodly conduct).

We could teach each other to respect our diversity!

We have all failed to practice ourselves the kind of behavior we expect from others.

We have to work together for the common good.

We need to focus on what we can do, not what we cannot do.

We need to make the best of the worst.

What we sow in thought, either useful or useless, manifests itself in our behavior.

Whatever people sow, that shall they reap. It can't be any other way.

When everyone does that which is right in his or her own eyes, who is right and who is wrong when there is disagreement?

When in doubt, just take the next small step.

When in doubt, tell the truth.

When temptations knock at our door, we should not ask them to stay for dinner.

When the battle is going well, we must not boast; when the battle is going hard, we must not despair.

When we admit our wrongs, it is as if a weight is lifted from us. We can breathe again normally.

Whenever we are wrong, we should admit it. Whenever we are right, we should shut up!

You cannot do wrong without suffering wrong.

Zealous people can do harm by wanting to impose their zeal and character on others.

BIBLE

A number of people portray a form of godliness that is contrary to Biblical truth; turn away from such people.

According to the Bible, marriage is an institution put in place by God, in which two adults of different gender choose to share an intimate, personal, and lasting relationship. Doing otherwise does not change this.

All lines of reasoning point toward the God of the Bible as the one, true God.

America evolved from a Biblical foundation. The majority of its residents have lost sight of this fact.

Best to obey the God of the Bible rather than self-proclaimed gods that are contrary to Scripture.

Biblical principles never change; they are the same "yesterday, today and forever."

Biblically, the greatest calling in the world is to serve others, as "The Servant" demonstrated.

Biblically, there is hope for even the most hopeless situations.

Biblically, we are responsible for ministering to one another's needs.

Culture emphasizes external (physical) beauty, which is destined to decrease; the Bible emphasizes internal (mental) beauty, which is destined to increase.

Every available source of information reveals that in religious matters, the majority has always been wrong (non-Biblical).

Getting satisfaction from giving to others is a Biblical concept.

In these days of relativism, situational ethics, and changing mores, it is good to know that we can count on Biblical principles that never change.

It does not come naturally to seek, obey, and then teach others the "Word of God" as recorded in the Bible.

It is impossible to rightly govern the world without God and the Bible. (George Washington)

It is not what we do not understand about the Bible that is a problem. It is what we do understand and do not do.

Love is the core message of the Bible.

Many books can inform, but only the Bible can transform.

Many people are guilty of pulling the Bible down to their level of understanding instead of bringing their level of understanding up to meet the requirements of the Word.

No book in the world deserves to be unceasingly studied and so profoundly meditated upon as the Bible.

Nothing in our culture is more restricted than the Word of God in Scripture.

Our present earthly life is temporary. The Bible states that we are just passing through on our way to a permanent home awaiting us in Heaven or Hell.

Society does us a big disservice when we go along with prioritizing people from most important to least important. This is not Biblical.

Stand up for what is Biblically right.

Test any prophecy, ancient or present, by whether or not it fully conforms to the Bible.

The Bible helps us put our life in proper perspective by directing us to focus on what matters most in life.

The Bible is God's love letter to us.

The Bible is not just a great book—it is THE Book! Its content is and will be forever. Those who abide by it are guaranteed salvation.

The Bible is the best source of "discipline that gives insight," and its wisdom can give shrewdness to the inexperienced ones and knowledge and thinking ability to a young man or woman.

The Bible teaches that every person has an important place in God's kingdom.

The Bible teaches that regardless of background, age, race, or any other factor, God loves everyone equally and desires a genuine, personal relationship with us.

The Bible tells us what will happen if we live by it and what will happen if we do not, no ifs, ands or buts.

The Bible's message includes love, mercy, forgiveness, kindness, justice, and reconciliation.

The faithful and obedient worship the God of the Bible alone.

The heart in the Bible is how we make contact with God and He with us.

The more we move away from Biblical principles, the less cohesive the world becomes.

The test for a right decision is to ask this question: Does it adhere to Biblical principles?

There are no demonstrable scientific errors in the Bible.

There is no book like the Bible from which more valuable lessons can be learned.

Violating Biblical principles leads to negative consequences.

We all need to have a purpose for living; the Bible gives us that purpose.

We can get by without any other book except the Bible.

We need a sound foundation like the Bible upon which to base our lives; unlike society, it does not drift, shift, or switch.

When desire and envy are not kept in check, they become our gods and supersede the God of the Bible.

When we decide to follow Biblical principles, the change will be gradual.

Whether people believe it or not, the Bible is the inerrant Word of God.

Worship the God of the Bible and serve Him first.

BLESSINGS

Biblical stewardship (trustee) is a way of living in which our blessings take on primary importance.

Bless those who curse you. Think what they would say if they knew the truth.

Blessings may be in plain sight or hidden behind clouds of anxiety and despair, but they are always part of our lives.

Diligent work and effort always precede fruitful blessings and rewards.

Find the bless in the mess.

Get rich quick: count your blessings.

God blesses us so that we can be a blessing to others.

No matter how low we feel, if we count our blessings, we will always show a profit.

People seldom count their blessings, such as a gain, goodness, and mercy.

People should use their blessings to bless others so all can benefit.

The longer we have been exposed to a particular blessing, the more likely we are to take it for granted.

The more we count the blessings we have, the less we crave the luxuries we do not have.

The presence of the Lord can be either a cause of fear or a source of blessing.

CHARACTER

Accountability is applicable to everyone because we reap what we sow.

Anything worth doing is worth doing well.

Attitude dictates our behavior.

Character is always sacrificed when one conforms to the culture that might differ.

Character is everything.

Character is much easier kept than recovered.

Character is what we are and do when nobody is looking.

Convert challenging situations into character-building opportunities.

EXPOSURE: Our character is molded by our surroundings.

Great character is developed in the crucible.

If there is righteousness (fairness) in the heart, there will be beauty in the character.

In the end, our choices shape our character and we receive what we give.

Our character is essentially the sum of our habits.

Scripture encourages people to be primarily concerned with spiritual matters, such as strength of character, honor, and good works.

The only thing that we take with us when we die is our character.

The world would be a much better place if the popular culture glamorized character rather than instant gratification.

View trying circumstances as character-building opportunities. This is much easier said than done.

We can remain content in our suffering knowing that suffering produces endurance, endurance produces character, character produces hope, and hope does not disappoint us.

When you need to choose the right course of action, just ask yourself what most people would do, and then do the opposite.

While most of us look at outward appearances, God looks at the heart (our inner disposition and character).

CHRISTIANITY

"And we know that all things work together for good to them that love God."

Acquiring understanding is critical; however, we must make sure that it is supported by Scripture and not the ever-changing culture.

All are not saints that go to church.

All eternal matters, such as forgiveness and salvation, are of infinitely greater value than the temporal things that occupy our minds.

Authentic worship results in action that confronts conditions, such as injustice, oppression, selfishness and greed.

Christian relationships are not only trustworthy with believers, but also with non-believers as well.

Christianity grows with love, not violence.

Christianity is not a religion but a relationship of love expressed toward God and people.

Christians can rejoice in tribulation because they have eternity's values in view.

Church is a fellowship where people care about others.

Church members and non-church individuals should focus on serving one another and their community.

Confession is good for the soul.

Do not wait for six strong men to take you to church.

False teachings (non-Biblical) lead to violence and cruelty. Eventually, they result in utter destruction.

Feed our souls and we will never go hungry.

Following God's Word results in obedience, which in turn brings joy to that person.

Friendship with the world (doing anything that conflicts with God's Word) is hatred toward God.

God gives us the courage to approach one another directly in Christian love, offer our concerns, listen to each other, and whenever possible, forgive.

God's word says that our lives are to be lived in service to one another.

Going to church doesn't make you a Christian any more than standing in a garage makes you a car.

Here is the conclusion of the matter: fear (revere) God and keep His Commandments.

If we are committed to studying Scripture, we are enlightened regarding God's word and we can also teach others.

In every age, men and women of faith are more often than not despised and persecuted by the world.

In God's presence we experience love, forgiveness, and acceptance.

Justification (right with God) is by grace through faith in Christ.

Lord, help me to be pure, but not yet!

Most of us tend to forget all God's benefits and fret over our troubles and burdens.

Only twenty percent of church members impact the lives of others.

Our love for Christ is only as real as our love for our neighbors.

Salvation has past, present, and future dimensions in all its aspects.

Salvation is by grace, not works, although genuine faith will surely produce good works.

Scripture informs us repeatedly that true and everlasting joy does not result from material wealth.

Scripture reminds us that we are to serve others, especially the needy.

Seven guiding principles to help nurture our faith in God's Word include justice, understanding, perseverance, endurance, reverence, friendship, and forgiveness.

Ten Commandments express God's love, will, and guidance concerning human conduct and relationships. They are the following:

1. You shall have no other gods before me.
2. You shall not make for yourself an idol.
3. You shall not take the name of the Lord your God in vain.
4. Remember the Sabbath day by keeping it holy.
5. Honor your father and your mother.
6. You shall not murder.
7. You shall not commit adultery.
8. You shall not steal.
9. You shall not give false testimony against your neighbor.
10. You shall not covet.

The Godly have so many true riches to enjoy: glory, goodness, grace, knowledge, mercy, and wisdom. It is so sad when so many try so desperately to acquire the uncertain riches of this world.

The habit of giving thanks and praise rather than complaint and criticism is a valuable Christian fruit.

The Lord declared: "For I know the plans I have for you – plans to prosper you and not to harm you, plans to give you hope and a future."

The national anthem of Hell is "I did it my way."

The time to repent is today, this very hour, and this very moment.

The word "love" means different things to different people. The Greek language is more specific: eros (sexual appeal); philia (friendship); storge (family members); agape (God's love for mankind and the love people are to have for one another).

This is the day the Lord has made; we will rejoice and be glad in it.

To abide in Christ means to continue believing His Word and serving Him.

To enter Heaven, we must take it with us.

We should be courageous Christians and seek out those who need help the most.

We should involve ourselves only in those things that will produce Christ-like purity, health, and joy in our lives.

When someone challenges our Biblical beliefs, we should not give up and we should not give in.

Without love, law-abidingness might become mechanical, miserable, and discouraging, but with love, every commandment inspires joy, delight, and peace of mind.

CONTENTMENT

A contented person has learned to accept the bitter with the sweet.

Contentment is an internal matter that is not at the mercy of external circumstances.

Contentment is living the virtues.

Contentment is one of the most precious gifts we can choose to experience and to wish for others.

Contentment must be appreciated in the present in order to experience it in the future.

Coveting and longing for something that is not ours produces much discontentment.

Discontented people soon become very lonely people.

Few people are modest enough to be content to be estimated at their true value.

It is not our circumstances that create our discontent or contentment. It is we.

Let our conversation be without covetousness; be content with such things as we have.

Real contentment must be based on what we are, not on what we would like to be.

Scripture teaches us that we are to be active in the world but not be of the world. We are to impact the world in a positive way and not have it impact us in a negative way. Some people are content to serve behind the scenes. Service is the important thing and not the notoriety.

Those who are discontented in one place will seldom be content in another.

True contentment is to enjoy the present without anxious dependence upon the future.

We are blessed with serenity when we are content with just who we are—no more, no less.

When our behavior limits covetousness, contentment abounds.

Young people yearn to be older, older people yearn to be younger, and many of those in-between are not sure one way or the other. The question becomes, "How much time remains to live contented lives?"

FAITH

A few people always prefer to believe the best of everybody; it saves so much trouble.

Amazing things can be accomplished when we resolve to live out our faith in unity.

Be a positive example in word, faith, purity, and actions.

Be strong and of good courage (faith) to cope in a dangerous world with all of its temptations and intimidations.

Belief comes before understanding and on this foundation understanding grows.

Belief is believing in something that cannot always be proved by reasoning.

Believers are to pursue spirituality that is authentic, compassionate, and just.

Believers prayerfully make decisions by seeking God's approval.

Believing we are of equal value in God's eyes would help free the world of hatred.

Biblical baptism requires choice, faith, repentance, and commitment on the part of the participant.

Biblical faith has proven itself to be the most powerful and enduring force in human history.

Faith does not suppress fear; what it does is allow us to go forward in spite of it.

Faith in God provides the power to love others unconditionally.

Faith is a matter of trusting God's promises.

Faith is belief in what we cannot see.

Faith is not about understanding; it is about trusting.

Faith is not being afraid of death, but embracing the true life that awaits us after we die.

Faith is refusing to panic.

Faith makes us move.

Faithfulness is our guide to salvation and an anchor for eternity.

Feed your faith and doubt will starve to death.

God has not called us to be successful; He has called us to be faithful.

God works through our words, actions, and relationships to bring good news to people by contrasting life without faith and life with faith.

God-abiding people need a strong faith, good courage, and much determination to face a dangerous world with all its temptations and intimidations.

God's law points out what is right, good, and true, and we are to live accordingly. Because of our sinful nature, however, we all fall short and our works cannot save us. This directs us to our need for grace. It is God's grace that makes salvation a reality for each faithful believer.

Have faith and pursue the unknown end.

If we seek to do God's will, our faith and our destiny can never be shaken.

In God's faithfulness lies eternal security.

Increasing our faith reduces our doubts.

It is very comforting to know and believe that we do not have to be like everybody else.

Scripture is not hard to understand; it is just hard to believe and even harder to obey.

The "owe me" attitude or belief that someone or some group owes us destroys gratitude.

The greatest blessings from "above" are the gifts of faith and hope and love.

The poor tend to be rich in faith and the rich tend to be poor in faith.

The question with God is not how obscure or prominent a place we occupy, but how faithful we are.

There is more honest faith in questioning than in silent resignation. Our faith must rest on the power of God.

There should be no difference between what people believe and their actions.

We choose each day what will be our goals and our legacy. Will people marvel at our achievements or give thanks for our faithful obedience, love, and grace?

We do well to keep the faith during life's journey. Our focus should be on areas of major importance and not quibble over incidental matters.

We have far more faith in material wealth these days than we do in God.

We should follow God's word faithfully, investing our time, talent and treasure in that which pleases Him.

What a person believes has everything to do with what a person becomes.

When we allow our anxieties rather than our faith to shape our lives, we tend to act with anger and foolishness.

Worry looks around; faith looks up.

FAMILY

A generation or two ago, children were taught that there was a Creator to whom they were responsible and to whom they had to answer in the afterlife. They were taught that a moral code was given to us to follow.

A mother cannot unlock all of life's doors for her children, but she can help them find the keys.

A parent's responsibility includes viewing every child without showing partiality.

Adolescents who identify their primary motives, such as helping others, are three times happier than those who lack such altruistic motivation.

All family members should express their concerns and explore options.

An important step in a young person's life is when he or she changes from parental dependence to Godly dependence. This point in one's journey of life will vary from person to person.

Anxiety about "looks" begins at a very early age. Parents should do their best to minimize this.

Any couple can birth a child, but it takes Godly parents to rear Godly children.

Anything parents can do to minimize procrastination in the children will reap great dividends in their later years.

As first teachers, parents must equip and enforce reasonable guidelines and parameters for their children; if they choose to deviate from that later, that is their prerogative.

As parents, the goal is not just to get children to obey, but to help them develop a healthy conscience—an internal sense of *right* and *wrong*.

As parents, we are to teach our children when we sit in our house, when we walk by the way, when we lie down, and when we rise up.

As the family weakens, so does the vertical transmission of family values. This promotes the horizontal transmission of values of the culture.

Blessings come in all shapes and sizes: a word of praise, a child's smile, or an answered prayer.

Breast-fed children and their mothers both benefit significantly over the non-nursing choices.

Cause-and-effect discipline with children really works.

Chances are children are going to worship the god of their parents, whoever or whatever it is.

Children benefit when the family eats together *without TV*.

Children growing up without a father are more likely to manifest undesirable behavior.

Children have no business having children. Check with those that have!

Children learn about accountability from their parents.

Children learn what they live!

Children must be taught to accept responsibility for their actions rather than make excuses and blame others.

Children need and require parental guidelines; expect them to grumble.

Children need clear boundaries: "This is allowed; this is not."

Children need good role models: girls need mothers and boys need fathers, if at all possible.

Children of all ages, but especially teenagers, need to know precisely what is expected of them and what the consequences of disobedience will be.

Children respond to their environment. It makes a big difference in how they turn out because it is recorded in their minds forever.

Children respond to tragedy differently. They look to adults for guidance on how they should react to grief. If adults absorb it and continue their lives, children assume they should do likewise.

Children tend to adopt their parents' attitudes very early in life.

Children thrive when parents devote individual attention to each child, if possible.

Children who become good at making excuses seldom become good at anything else.

Children who grow up without responsibilities learn to live a lazy life.

Children, especially boys, should be older than the average rather than younger when they start school.

Divorce is more difficult for children to cope with than the death of a parent, and it lingers forever.

Every child has his or her own bent. It is best not to compare them.

Family discussions are better when everybody faces one another.

Family relationships and responsibilities are of great importance to God.

Generally speaking, children should be limited to the cash allowance allotted them.

Giving children allowances is one way to begin teaching them how to save money and budget for the things they might want.

God holds parents responsible for teaching their children right from wrong.

Good things happen when families eat their meals together.

Having a child to improve the marriage relationship is a poor reason to embark upon parenthood.

Having fun together as a family is a key part of building a strong family identity.

If children do not learn to obey their parents, chances are they will not obey any other authority.

If children live with acceptance and friendship, they learn to practice love in the world.

If we are not happy single, we will not be happy married. The same principle applies to having children.

In most households, this is the first time in history that parents are no longer the main influence in child rearing.

In raising children, like everything else, what we do speaks so much louder than what we say. The challenge is to narrow the gap between word and deed.

It is a good thing to encourage children to do things for their parents.

It is a known fact that most children will follow in their parents' footsteps and so will the generations that follow.

It is better to make a child stretch to reach your high opinion than stoop to match your disrespect.

It is natural for youth to assume they are safe and for parents to worry about them.

It seldom occurs to teenagers that some day they will know as little as their parents.

It takes patience, perseverance, and quality time to raise responsible children.

Kids need a hero. There is no one more suited than a close, caring, and loving adult.

More parents need to have sound, well-thought-out rules regarding childrearing and stick to them.

Most young people tend to listen more to their peers than their seniors.

Nations go downhill when families go downhill. History does not document one civilization that survived without a dominating number of morally strong families.

No family challenge is impossible with loving help.

No parents are perfect; therefore, children (as adults) must *learn* to *unlearn* and then *relearn.*

Nurturing surfaces during parenting, caring, and mentoring. Relying on Biblical principles helps distinguish between what is right and what is wrong.

Obedience in children is one of the most important responsibilities of parenting.

Our children get only one childhood. Make it a good one.

Our kids are becoming us!

Overly demanding parents do not take into consideration the thoughts, feelings, and needs of their children.

Overweight children and adults tend to rationalize their condition rather than question their eating habits.

Parents are the first and most influential teachers their children will ever have.

Parents are to bring up their children to love and obey the Lord, especially by their example and spoken words.

Parents are ultimately responsible for how their children turn out.

Parents implant the knowledge of God's Word; they should not rely on a substitute to do it.

Parents must be heads of the household while ruling with love.

Parents need the help of others to raise their children. "It takes a village to raise a child."

Parents need to be cautious about trying to make their children carbon copies of themselves.

Parents need to encourage their children to learn from their mistakes and then forget them.

Parents should avoid comparing their children with other children, especially their brothers and sisters.

Parents should help their child think about the character traits for which he or she would like to be known.

Parents who do not allow their children to experience failure or sadness give them a false view of the world and do not prepare them for the harsh realities of the adult life.

Parents who do not discipline their children do not love them.

Parents who encourage their children to set goals and go after them deserve an A+.

Parents, provoke not your children to wrath, but bring them up in the nature and admonition of the Lord.

People who insult others (especially children) inflict wounds that never heal completely.

Poor communication is at the root of most family problems.

Praise your children openly; reprove them secretly.

Protecting young people from risky behaviors and helping them develop positive behavior are easier when parents spend quality time together as a family.

Research tells us that the average adult needs seven to nine hours (more for children) of sleep nightly; our quality of life depends on it.

Some teenagers ignore rules in order to see what they can get away with. They might test the boundaries to see if parents will follow through. Being consistent is crucial.

Striving to eliminate sinful patterns in our lives is most praiseworthy; however, the ultimate objective is being obedient children of God.

Teens who are givers are not only happier, but also they are more excited about life and more involved at school and with their families. They also are less likely to fail a subject in school, get pregnant, or abuse substances.

The biggest secret to being a happy family is just trying.

The costs and benefits of expanded preschool is not the answer to our educational problems because it does not get to the root of the cause, which is inadequate parenting.

The louder parents speak to their children, the less they listen.

The more children know about their family history, the stronger their sense of control over their lives and the higher their self-esteem.

The most highly charged time of day for a family is between 6:00 p.m. and 8:00 p.m.

The most important thing that a father can do for his children is to love their mother.

The reason many parents no longer lead their children in the right direction is because they are not going that way themselves.

The sooner parents expect responsible behavior from their children, the sooner they will come through.

The strongest self-worth develops in children who perceive unconditional love from their parents.

They who bring trouble to their family will inherit only wind.

Those who still have parents should express their love and show respect while there still is time, for it is later than we think.

Train children in the way they should go, and when they mature, they will not depart from it.

Unfortunately, most people have little or no education on how to be a good husband, wife, or parent in comparison to job education and training.

We should mean what we say or not say it, particularly with children.

What a mother sings to the cradle goes all the way down to the coffin.

What parents pass on to their children will be passed on to their children, who then will pass it on to children yet unborn.

When parents eat sour grapes, their children's teeth chatter.

When parents spend time with their children, they pay them the highest compliment they will ever receive.

Young children should have no authority over their parents.

Young people are often ignorantly thoughtless, as a rule.

Young people can really benefit by capitalizing on the experience of more mature individuals.

Youngsters and the inexperienced (ignorant) would do well to seek the advice of older people; chances are they have been there.

FORGIVENESS

Being slow to criticize and quick to forgive is a good way to go.

Even though we are sinful, Jesus' mercy, forgiveness, and love are there to heal us, save us, and send us out with the "good news."

Forgiveness frees and heals the forgiver as well as the forgiven.

Forgiveness is not an occasional act. It is an attitude.

Forgiveness is the highest and most beautiful form of love.

Forgiving ourselves is just as important as forgiving others.

Forgiving someone is not necessarily doing something for someone else, although that can be a possibility; it is more a gift we give to ourselves that allows us to move forward with our lives.

God has blessed every "believer" with forgiveness of sin and eternal life.

God is "ready to forgive" everyone. He will never turn away those who approach Him with repentant hearts.

God is a super-forgiver for super-sinners.

God's word directs us to choose love over hate, forgiveness over scorekeeping, and mercy over judgment.

If we confess our sins, God is just and will forgive us our sins and purify us from all unrighteousness.

Our self-centeredness is reduced in direct proportion to our giving and forgiving attitude.

Praise be to God in whose presence there is acceptance, forgiveness, harmony, healing, peace, salvation, and wholeness.

Sin cannot be undone, only forgiven.

The gift of eternal life is ours today. It includes God's love, forgiveness, and new life.

The harder it is for us to forgive, the further we are from true love.

The key to a good marriage is having two good forgivers.

We have sinned against God in thought, word, and deed by what we have done and by what we have left undone. We have not loved Him with our whole heart; we have not loved our neighbor as ourselves. We need to ask forgiveness and thank Him for being our Lord and Savior.

We need to break through the barrier that hinders forgiveness.

When God forgives us, our sins are forgotten.

FRIENDSHIP

A friend hangs in there with his or her friend.

A good friend is cheaper than therapy.

Do I not destroy my enemies by making them my friends?

Friends are those rare people who ask how you are and wait for an answer.

Friends are those who do not use one another for a selfish purpose.

Friends are very important to have. First be one.

Friends should bear their friends' infirmities.

Friendship and unconditional acceptance bring out the best in us.

If each of us would reach out in caring friendship to one person today, what a difference it would make for us all.

Many young "gamers" choose video games over friendships.

Only a real friend will tell you when your face is dirty.

Reprove a friend in secret but praise him or her before others.

The time to make friends is before we need them.

To find a friend one must close one eye. To keep a friend, one must close two.

Who seeks a faultless friend remains friendless.

GIVING

Attention towards the needs of others is a healthy sign.

Be generous with praise. Be cautious with criticism and overcome it with goodness.

Be one who looks for the best in others and give them the best you have.

Generous behavior reduces adolescent depression and suicide. Several studies have shown that teenagers who do volunteer work are less likely to fail a subject in school, get pregnant, or abuse substances.

Give not advice without being asked; and when desired, do it briefly.

Give the gift of your absence to those who do not appreciate you.

Give the world the best we have. We could get hurt, but give it anyway.

Giving doesn't come easily, and that is why most people struggle with "It is more blessed to give than receive."

Gratitude and humility rather than resentment and grumbling should characterize our handling of circumstances that arise in everyday living.

Helping others enhances our feelings of self-worth.

If we give what we do not need, it is not giving.

In our world of plenty, it seems easier than ever to lose sight of what is truly important.

It is mainly in our giving that the harvest will be realized.

Many people feel detached from others because they are all of the time *taking in* and never *giving out*.

Nobody needs a smile so much as those who have none left to give.

Often God calls on us to give of ourselves in selfless ways so others may learn from our example.

People lean heavily towards getting rather than giving.

Personal gifts should not be prioritized because they are all needed by someone.

Seven Biblical paradoxes that relate to basic truth are the following: To get, we must give; To really live, we must die; To save one's life, he or she must lose it; To be wise, we must become fools; To reign, we must serve; To be exalted, we must become humble; To be first, we must be last.

The generous eye and the generous attitude are the basis of sound human relationships.

They are no fool who give what they cannot keep to gain what they cannot lose.

Time is the most valuable gift one can give.

To get or to give? That is the question. Here then is the secret of an abundant life: to give is to live and to live is to give.

Unless life is lived for others as well, it is not worthwhile.

We cannot give to others what we do not possess.

When it comes to giving, some people stop at nothing.

When we give little to a relationship, we should not expect much in return.

GOD

A feeble compromise between Godly and worldly will satisfy neither.

A person of God, doing the will of God, is immortal until his or her work is done.

A policy of separation of church and state is totally different from separation of God and state.

Acknowledge and delight in God's present and future promise.

All God really wants from us is our attention.

All motives become known and weighed by God.

All of our decisions and undertakings should be compatible with Godly standards.

All Scripture is God-breathed and is useful for teaching, rebuking, correcting, and training in righteousness.

All service ranks the same with God.

All things in God's time.

All things work together for good to they that love God. This is one of God's most difficult promises to believe in in times of affliction and loss.

Any decision, other than those acceptable to God, is the wrong decision.

Any person who endeavors to live a Godly life is bound to encounter opposition.

As God's representatives, we should make it our goal to influence as many people as possible in a positive direction.

As humans, we have the potential to reflect God's personality traits, such as love, justice, and wisdom.

Ask God each day to give you the thoughts, words, and actions to help you along the way.

Be anxious about nothing; give it to God.

Be not ignorant of this one thing—that one day is with the Lord as a thousand years, and a thousand years is as one day.

Be not wise in your own eyes; fear (revere) God and turn away from evil.

Because God is with us, we can help make the world a better place.

Because of the culture, a small minority of us consider ourselves as beautiful or handsome. The large majority of us are considered plain, unattractive, or ugly. God views us all as being beautiful and handsome.

Behind and beyond events we cannot comprehend is God, who cares for us personally and passionately.

Best to obey Scripture (God's Word) than any other declared authority.

Blaming God for our troubles is like being on a dead-end street. It doesn't take you anywhere.

Blessed are all that put their trust in God.

Blessed is the person who walks not in the counsel of the ungodly.

By God's grace, we are blessed to be a blessing to others, thereby revealing God's glory.

Come near to God and He will come near to you.

Compromise has become the order of the day. God's people are choosing to conform to the ways of the world and hold on to God and His principles at the same time. This cannot be done. In time, the consequences will bear this out.

Conversations in which people disagree yet respect one another are rare. Hopefully, God's presence would be felt on both sides of the divide.

Do not give me your list to live by and I will not give you mine; instead, follow God's list.

Do not tell God how big our storms are; tell the storms how big our God is.

Draw near to God and He will draw near to you.

Each of us is a unique expression God's loving design.

Each of us will give an account of himself or herself to God.

Each one of us lacks God's spirit at birth; it must be sought and claimed as we mature to the age of reason.

Enthusiasm for God is contagious. Has anyone caught it from you?

Even when a wrongdoer is successful keeping a transgression a secret, God knows.

Every day contains the possibility for a life-transforming encounter with God through some unanticipated new connection.

Every word of God is pure. He is a shield for those who put their trust in Him.

Everyone who calls on the Lord shall be saved and blessed.

Exercise daily—walk with God.

Fear thrives when God's presence is absent; peace thrives when God's presence is present.

Feeding on God's Word increases our appetite for it.

For direction, let God's Word fill our memory, rule our heart, and guide our life.

For those who love God, all things work together for good.

For whosoever shall call upon the name of the Lord shall be saved. This is one of God's greatest promises.

Giving thanks and praising God for our many blessings should be an ongoing act.

God alone is totally worthy of all our devotion and praise.

God always offers us that which is best for us.

God answers to knee mail.

God calls us according to the gifts He has given us.

God can and does change people in small and big ways. The ones we view as least likely will most likely surprise us.

God can change us from a life of self-centeredness to one of God-centeredness.

God can make a nobody somebody.

God can restore us and does not count our trespasses against us.

God can take our weakness, if we give it to Him, and turn it into strength that will glorify Him and benefit us.

God can turn any difficulty into an opportunity.

God comes to all who seek Him with all their heart and soul and mind.

God considers the honoring of parents by their children to be of great importance; it is vital if our children are to come also to honor their Heavenly Father.

God created us free moral agents, which enables us to choose right over wrong and to express our love for others in a variety of ways.

God does not abandon us in our distress; He sticks with us through thick and thin.

God does not abandon us when we do foolish and stupid things.

God does not get angry with the people that anger us.

God does not leave us where we are.

God expects from us what a healthy parent expects of a toddler learning to walk.

God forbids favoritism of any kind except His word.

God gives each his or her due at the time allotted.

God has a record of everything.

God heals us of those illnesses that prevent us from becoming the people He wants us to become.

God instructs, we obey, and He performs.

God is available to heal what we often conceal.

God is first and He is last! We are gathered up in between, as in great arms of an eternal, loving kindness.

God is on our side as long as we are on His side and follow his clearly revealed Word.

God isn't interested in changing our circumstances; He wants to change our character.

God knows and cares about us regardless of how we feel about ourselves.

God knows that His likeness resonates in the human heart, drawing honest-hearted people to Him and setting them on the path to everlasting life.

God knows us and desires to be known by us and calls us to dwell in His presence.

God loves the rich, the poor, and everybody in between.

God loves us with even greater love than we can even imagine.

God never consults your past to determine your future.

God of grace and glory, guide us into unity with all for the sake of the whole world.

God of time and space is a caring, trusting, and personal God.

God offers salvation and we can either accept it or reject it and live with the consequences.

God often speaks in a still and small voice and works in quiet ways.

God opposes the proud (arrogant) but gives grace to the humble (knowing and correcting one's weaknesses and faults).

God opposes the proud and gives grace to the humble.

God permits what He hates; hopefully, we choose to learn from these destructive circumstances.

God promises a safe landing, not a calm passage.

God reminds us that He is able to meet all of our needs of every sort.

God reproves the ones He loves; this same principle is just as applicable to parents rearing children.

God *sees* everything, *hears* everything, and *knows* everything.

God sends His message through His servants.

God should occupy the supreme position in our hearts.

God shows no partiality and welcomes everyone.

God values each one of us as equal.

God wants each of us to reflect His light by loving others the way He loves each of us.

God wants us to deal with ourselves even more so than with others.

God wants us to live in simple obedience to His will as stated in His Word, by proclaiming it in all that we think, say, and do.

God wants us to live in simple obedience to His Word in all that we think, say, and do.

God welcomes us into a kingdom of peace that passes all human understanding.

God will grant eternal life to His redeemed followers.

God will judge everyone's deeds, including every hidden thing, whether good or evil.

God's command is that we should believe Jesus and love one another.

God's commandments remove the confusion about right and wrong in today's relativistic culture, protect us from the consequences of our own moral weaknesses, and guide our thinking and actions in every situation.

God's focus never decreases. His love for us never diminishes.

God's gifts to each of us should make us more conscious of our limited worthiness and more appreciative of His grace.

God's grace is strong enough to counter every worldly circumstance.

God's great gift of salvation, though faintly understood now, is a gift of love, grace, peace, and joy.

God's healing love is the balm that eases the pain of life's hurts and gives a joy and purpose we could never have without Him.

God's law has not changed because God does not change.

God's love for us is unconditional and our love for others should be the same.

God's love is for everyone—no exception! All we have to do is believe and accept it.

God's truth is not determined by taking a vote or by the opinions of skeptics.

God's way of life is the way of love and giving which yields happiness, joy, and peace.

God's ways are not the ways of the world. He makes those who appear to be last in the world first in His Kingdom.

God's Word gives us the discernment to distinguish between "good-right and evil-wrong."

God's Word says the harder we work to serve others and promote the "give" way, the more we will grow and the more we will "receive in return."

Godless people are more inclined to be lovers of themselves, lovers of money, boastful, proud, abusive, disobedient to their parents, ungrateful, unholy, without love, unforgiving, slanderous, without self-control, brutal, not lovers of good, treacherous, rash, conceited, and lovers of pleasure rather than lovers of God.

Godly living produces love, joy, and peace in one's life.

Godly principles are scarcely followed in high places.

Good character is what we look for in others. It is what employers look for in us and, most importantly, this is what God looks for in us. How we accomplish something should always have priority over what we accomplish.

Good stewardship involves submitting all our resources to God's authority.

Grace means God accepts us just as we are.

How we perceive ourselves marks the ceiling for what God can do for us.

Hymns of praise remind us that God is as close as the sound of our voices singing together.

If God calls us to do it, He will pull us through it!

If God controls us on the inside, we will be genuine on the outside.

If the word of culture differs from the Word of God, the culture should get trumped.

If there is disagreement between what the secular world says and what God says, there is no contest.

If there is something in our life keeping us from hearing God, we should confront it.

If we are not careful, pride, security, cowardice, wealth and reputation can become our gods.

If we claim to believe God, our actions should represent him accurately.

If we keep in step with God, we probably will be out of step with the world.

If we keep our eyes on God, we won't lose sight of life's purpose.

If we labor in God's kingdom, our names will appear in the "Book of Life."

If we would use the power that God gives us to see ourselves as others see us, it would free us from many a blunder and foolish notion.

In God's eyes, none of us is a failure without hope.

In God's presence our understanding changes for good.

In the beginning was the Word, and the Word was with God, and the Word was God.

It does not come naturally to seek, obey, and then teach others the words of God as found in Scripture.

It does not make any difference who gets the praise as long as God gets the glory.

It is a deadly mistake to follow those who choose worldly ways over Godly ways.

It is difficult to always do what is right because we tend to trust in ourselves rather than God.

It is God's free gift of grace that justifies us (declares us righteous).

It is God's love for us that makes it possible for us to love God and others.

It is not all about getting recognition for utilizing our gifts; it is for God's glory.

It is of very little account what people think of us, but it is of vast importance what God thinks of us.

It is possible that the most significant acts of all are carried out in secret, seen by no one but God.

It is so easy to become so involved in our own plans that God's direction is hidden from our view.

It pleases God when His word is honored, obeyed, and taught.

Keeping our minds on Godly expectations is not easy.

Know and seek God in every situation, then follow your dreams by trusting in His guidance.

Let God's promises shape our attitudes.

Life is good, but its purpose isn't clear apart from God.

Life is the gift of God and enjoyed most by those who obey God's commandments.

Life not centered in God is without purpose and meaning.

Love of people leads to love of God and the opposite is even truer.

Love the Lord your God with all your heart and with all your soul and with all your mind. This is the first and greatest commandment, and the second is like it. Love your neighbor as yourself.

Loving God produces obedience, which in turn brings joy in that obedience.

Many people have hidden agendas; God does not.

Many tend to remember God more in times of anguish, sorrow, or fear than in times of joy.

May we express God's love to the people around us every day.

More and more people are drifting way from God's Word.

Most people are missed about as long as it takes water to settle after it splashes in a bucket. Not so with God.

Most people find it difficult not to be anxious, fearful and worried about life's trials. Godly faith and trust promise us many blessings, not the least of which is peace.

Most people view others as self-centered or God-centered.

Most people wish to serve God, but only in an advisory capacity.

No eye has seen, nor ear heard, nor the human heart conceived, what God has prepared for those who love Him.

No life is pleasing to God that is not useful and beneficial to people.

No one has our unique design; therefore, everyone is different but of equal value in God's eyes.

Now is the time to embrace grace, the love and favor that God shows toward people even though they don't deserve it.

Obedience to God's commandments is an expression of our love for Him.

Obedience to God's instructions requires great effort, but He gives us samples of comfort, encouragement, and hope.

One of the greatest favors God can bestow upon us is the knowledge of His Word.

One of the greatest steps in discovering who we are is discovering who God is.

One on God's side is a majority.

One-on-one relationships are top priority with God.

Only God is worthy of true worship.

Only God's inspired word can protect us against the deception of our enemies.

Our behavior can encourage or discourage unbelievers to seek God's way of living.

Our challenge is to learn to "trust and obey" God's Word.

Our curiosity should focus on the Word of God.

Our experiences should be consistent with Godly principles.

Our faith helps us to believe that God is love.

Our hearts are restless until they rest with God.

Our hearts are restless until we establish a personal relationship with God.

People are judged by God according to their actions and works.

People are much more inclined to embrace "the spirit of the world" than "the spirit of God."

People are responsible for planting good seed and not responsible for how others respond; that is God's job.

People never violate God's laws without suffering the consequences sooner or later.

People often focus on God's "prohibitions" (negative) rather than His "provisions" (positive).

People who keep God's commandments dwell in Him and He in them.

People who preface their remarks with "honest to God" tend to lie.

People who revere God will avoid worldly extremes.

Pride leads to every other vice; it is the complete anti-God state of mind.

Problems in the world will only intensify and become worse without adherence to God's law.

Reputation is what people think of us; character is what God knows of us.

Returning good for good is human; returning good for evil is divine.

Sanctity is always choosing the will of God.

Seek God and call upon Him regarding all matters.

Society is increasingly drifting away from God's Word.

Take the time to build a relationship with God.

Thank God for His loving hands until at last we are homeward bound.

The church building is not where we find God. The church is anywhere God is obeyed and worshipped.

The deeper we stoop to God, the deeper we stoop to serve others.

The end goal is to "display ourselves" as those who are approved by God.

The end results of obeying God's commandments are peace, joy, and contentment.

The eyes of the Lord are in every place, keeping watch on the evil and the good.

The fear [reverence] of God is the beginning of knowledge, but fools despise wisdom and discipline.

The formula for unending joy is putting God first, others second, and one's self third.

The founders of our nation never intended to exclude God-of-the-Bible from the classroom and government because they knew that society needed a firm and proven foundation upon which to base its system of values. The fact that the United States went from the least to most esteemed nation in the world proves that they were right. Why would anyone want to change a proven plan?

The fruit [blessings] of the Holy Spirit is love, joy, peace, patience, kindness, goodness, faithfulness, gentleness and self-control.

The God of the Bible is Father, Son, and Holy Spirit and I put my faith in Him.

The highest goal is learning to know God.

The Lord requires the following from us: do justly, love mercy and walk humbly with God.

The Lord's commandments are clear and provide light so the eyes can see.

The more "stuff" we have in our life, the less room there is for God's influence.

The more we learn about God and imitate him, the more we live the way He intended us to live. As a result, we experience more joy in life, along with genuine satisfaction, inner peace, and contentment.

The most acceptable service we render God is service to His children.

The motivation for our actions should be to glorify God, not to gain personal praise.

The only way through grief is to grieve. We must work through the pain of whatever the circumstances.

The secular world is tangible; God's world is intangible.

The way to be self-controlled is to be God-controlled.

The wisdom of God's word not only informs us as to what is right, but also it transforms us into His image.

The word of God provides the light we need to find our way in life.

There are just two possible ways of life: God's way (good), expressed by His law of love, peace, and joy – the "give" way; and Satan's way (bad), as reflected in competition, greed, and violence – the "get" way.

There are many paths up the mountain of God.

There are three major influences that impact our lives: circumstances, people, and God's Word (or its absence). Whatever the influence, anything contrary to God's Word should be rejected.

There are two kinds of people: those who say to God, "Thy will be done" and those to whom God says, "All right then, have it your way."

There is a big difference in hoping for *something* and hoping *in someone* like God.

There is always more to learn and God knows what we are ready to hear.

There is more to life than impressing others with our possessions, intellect, or talents. To those who "believe" in God, we have been given life over death.

There is new hope in God every day.

There is no real purpose to life without God; otherwise, it is all about "me."

There must be an authorized chain-of-command in any church body or other organizations for them to functions responsibly. The key is loyalty to God's Word.

Things go better when people live God-fearing (reverent) lives.

This the day the Lord has made; let us rejoice and be glad in it.

Those who delight in God's ways will grow, thrive, and bring forth good fruit.

Those who have God's peace within them can thrive within strife.

Those who know and love God have a friend who is with them always.

Those who seek first the kingdom of God and His righteousness has the promise that God will supply all their earthly needs.

Those who seek God are brought into His presence.

Time is a precious gift of God, so precious that it is only given to us moment by moment.

True morality is generated internally from a heart of gratitude and love for God and His Word.

Trust in the Lord with all your heart and lean not on your own understanding.

Unique gifts (talents, abilities, treasures) have been given to each of us to be used for God's purpose of making the world a better place for everyone.

Unity prevails where God's presence prevails.

Unless the Lord builds the house [any undertaking], its builders labor in vain.

Unlike many of us, God does not have a hidden agenda.

We all come into God's family one at a time.

We are called to love and serve others, but above that, we are called to love and serve God.

We are children of God, made in His image, and valued in His sight.

We are God's stewards (managers) entrusted by Him with our time, talents, and treasures. Also, we are responsible for the proper use of the earth's resources.

We are more inclined to follow or own deeply cherished desires or long-entrenched attitudes than the word of God.

We are not only to receive God's grace for ourselves, but also we must dispense it to others.

We are to obey God, not just because He tells us to, but also because it will benefit us in the long run.

We can never lose our way if we abide with God each day.

We can only see the tip of the iceberg when viewing a person; only God can see and know the complete person—heart, mind and soul.

We do not change God's message. His message changes us.

We enter God's kingdom by birth. This means a person voluntarily chooses the "second" (spiritual) birth.

We have authority over our thoughts, but God does not force us to exercise this aspect of our free will.

We know that we have come to know God if we obey His commandments.

We must make it a point to help rather than condemn those who do not abide in God's Word.

We must not be swayed by the perverse reasoning of the "politically correct world." We must allow God's Word to guide us.

We need faith and courage to live as God's people and do the work we are called on to do.

We need to confess our lack of trust in God's mercy.

We need to make an effort to express God's love to the people around us each day.

We often hear it said, "If God existed, there would be no wars." It would be truer to say, "If God's laws were observed, there would be no wars."

We ought not go along with cultural proclamations that conflict with Godly truth.

We rise to the confidence level that we have in our God.

We should be at peace and thank God for all of our blessings.

We should do our best to present ourselves to God as approved according to His Word.

We should do our very best to view others as God views them.

We should not allow anything to separate us from the love of God.

We should recount all of our blessings and share our burdens with God.

We should remain steadfast in God's principles of right and wrong.

We should strive to make God's priorities our priorities and try our best to think as He does on every issue.

We should want to know and follow God's commandments because they are just and holy, and not because we might gain salvation by them.

We were bought at a price; therefore, we ought to glorify God with healthy bodies and pure minds.

We were created to have a personal relationship with the God of the Bible, not worldly "gods." Each person must choose and live with the consequences.

What God gives us, He expects us to share with others.

Whatever God wills endures forever; nothing can be added to it, nothing can be taken from it.

When "the faith" is passed on, God's blessings endure from generation to generation. The opposite is also true.

When our trust is focused on God, we are more likely to be led by His will, through thick and thin.

When we are self-centered, we cannot be God-centered, and the opposite is just as true.

When we choose not to follow God, He does not abandon us, but does allow us to go our own way.

When we walk God's path and dwell in His light, there is truly no darkness.

Whether we are called to be leaders or followers of God, each of us must be willing and able to "endure the challenges."

Will the road you are on get you to my place? —God.

With God, it is never too late to pick up the pieces and rebuild.

With God's help we have the power to encourage or discourage, to motivate or deflate, to generate joy or repel it. These are very realistic possibilities.

Worldly pleasures of our choosing can crowd God out of our lives.

Worry is when we trust our fears more than we trust God.

GOVERNMENT

A nation without means to reform is without means of survival.

A truly moral nation enacts policies that encourage personal responsibility and discourage self-destructive behavior by not subsidizing people who live irresponsibly and make poor choices. And because someone else pays the bill, the behavior continues and gets worse.

Bad government is better than no government.

Government cannot afford welfare programs for able-bodied people who make unwise choices and expect other people to pay for them; plus, it promotes irresponsibility.

Human government without God is like building on a foundation of sand.

If people were angels, no government would be necessary.

Our system of democracy cannot survive with ignorant and uncaring citizens who can easily be manipulated by "slick" politicians.

Today, more and more of our elected representatives in government are of questionable loyalty; often they focus on personal gain rather than promoting the common good.

We are doing away with some of the very things, such as Biblical principles, that have made America the greatest nation in the world.

When the political party becomes more important than the "principle," the whole country suffers.

GRATITUDE

Being gracious is difficult. It could mean letting go of grudges and prejudices and going beyond what is fair to what is merciful.

For today and its blessings, we owe the world an attitude of gratitude.

Gratitude and humility rather than resentment and grumbling should characterize our handling of circumstances that arise in everyday living.

Gratitude is a conscious and deliberate decision to focus on life's blessings rather than its shortcomings.

Gratitude is a conviction, a practice, and a discipline that benefits everyone.

Proud people are seldom grateful because they seldom think they get as much as they deserve.

Stop and find at least one thing in life for which you can be grateful.

There is something in every season to celebrate with thanksgiving.

GREED

Greed is a human weakness present in all societies.

In God we trust. This appears on our money and is our national motto.

Inside each of us is a degree of greed, dishonesty, pride, hatred, and selfishness.

Investing our minds and our interests as we would our money in worthwhile activities will generate long-term dividends.

It is not the person who has little that is poor; it is he who desires more.

It is wise and beneficial to refrain from all kinds of sin (wrongs), especially those that produce deadly consequences in everyday living. Examples are the following: MONEY, the *love* of money meaning gain at any cost is a good thing; IDOLATRY, worshipping created things more than the Creator God; FORNICATION, premarital sex that is degrading and often results in sexual disease and abortion.

Money is good; it is the love of money that is bad.

Money is the number one topic about which husbands and wives argue.

Money lovers are seldom satisfied with their income.

Money management reveals our true virtues.

Never spend your money before you have it.

No bees, no honey; no work, no money.

Obviously, in order to save money, we have to spend less than we make.

Often we use our God-given gifts to our own end, rather than share them.

Pleasure-craze behavior, such as drug abuse, gambling, overspending, promiscuous sex, and sports, are cause for grave concern.

The prevailing spirit of today's society includes self-indulgence, lust, greed, materialism, excess, cheating, and pride. All are sinful and transgress God's law.

To manage money and enjoy the process, give ten percent, save ten percent, and live on the remaining eighty percent.

When people gamble, the more they play, the more they lose.

When people say, "It's not the money, it's the principle," it is usually the money.

HATE

A lie told often enough could become known as truth.

According to research, people benefit when their positive emotions outnumber negative ones by three to one.

As people advance in years, many wish they had not done certain negative things; instead, they wished they had done more positive things when the opportunity arose.

As we feed our minds with positive thoughts, the negative ones will be displaced.

Hate is like acid. It can damage the vessel in which it is stored as well as destroy the object on which it is poured.

Hate is not the opposite of love—indifference is.

Hating people is like taking poison and hoping *they* die.

Hatred causes destruction; love causes construction.

Hostility and lack of appreciation stifle and squelch the human spirit.

Individual disobedience can have extended, negative consequences.

It is hard to hate people when you're doing something good for them.

Love must be sincere. Hate what is evil; cling to what is good.

More law abiding results in *less* crime, violence, and destruction.

Negative expressions convey "stinkin' thinkin.'"

Never let an old wound fester due to excessive attention.

Once a word (negative or positive) is stated, it may very well become reality.

People are more inclined to focus on negative circumstances than positive ones.

Positive everything is better than negative nothing.

Positive thinking helps us do everything better than negative thinking will.

Replacing negative thoughts with positive ones puts us on the "right" road.

The only way to eliminate negative or counter-productive thoughts is to replace them with positive, empowering thoughts.

The power of habit causes us to express the negative and ignore the positive.

There are guaranteed negative consequences for shirking one's responsibilities.

Those who say, "I love God," and hate their brothers or sisters are liars, for those who do not love a brother or a sister whom they have seen cannot love God whom they have not seen.

Too much of anything has negative consequences.

We can do away with the negative thought only when we replace it with a positive thought.

We can experience our free will by choosing either positive or negative courses of action.

We need public outcry and political rage over violence in America to fix our depraved culture.

Whatever we do has everlasting consequences, positive or negative.

When the need arises to express anger, hate, or revenge, we should do it privately and not publicly.

You must accentuate the positive, eliminate the negative, and do not mess with "Mr. In-Between."

HEALTH

According to recent studies, physical and mental activities help reduce weight, high blood pressure, heart disease, depression, sadness, stress, and more; plus, people's outlooks on life become more positive.

According to the U.S. Surgeon General, nearly ninety percent of smokers start by age eighteen. The smoking habit guarantees serious physical harm to everyone, not to mention the expense over a lifetime.

Eating a high amount of natural, whole grains and low amounts of processed foods puts one on a path of optimal health.

Exercise will keep our energy level high, strengthen our immunity, improve our mood, and reduce the effects of negative stress, to name a few benefits.

Gardening has social and mental health benefits as well as fresh air and bright skies; it also provides good exercise.

Hand washing plays a major role in protecting one's health.

Healthy living means keeping an eye on the future.

It is physical and mental health that is the real wealth in our lives.

Now and then, it is good to distinguish between our needs and our wants. Needs are food, water, shelter, and clothing.

Physical activity is among the healthiest things we can do for ourselves. Studies tell us that "taking it easy" is a real danger.

Spiritual hunger is never satisfied with material food.

HOPE

Each one of us hopes for something. Hope gives us the strength to keep going in the face of need, great or small. Hope is essential to life.

Hope lights a candle instead of cursing the darkness.

Hope sees the invisible, feels the intangible, and achieves the impossible.

Often people vainly pursue hopes and expectations that, in reality, are meaningless.

Without hope it is extremely difficult to take the next step.

JESUS

A new commandment I give you: Love one another as I have loved you. Each of us is called to follow the example of Jesus.

A person needs to acknowledge his or her sinful nature before coming to Christ for salvation.

All who drink from the wells of the world will thirst again, but just a single drink from the springs of living water of which Christ spoke eliminates spiritual thirst forever.

Anticipation is a significant part of the excitement of Jesus' return.

Anyone desiring forgiveness of sin and eternal salvation must come to God through Jesus Christ.

Being in Christ frees us from judgment, since He has already borne our judgment.

Believers are not to be selfish or proud but followers of Jesus: humble, obedient, and servants.

Christ wants us to approach Him with a feeling of joy and self-worth.

Christian Gospel is what only Jesus proclaimed. All other proclamations are false.

Christmas is strictly about Jesus, the real reason for the season.

Easter is celebrating Jesus paying our debt.

Either people believe in Jesus for salvation or they do not. There is no middle ground between heaven and hell.

Eternal peace and righteousness will become reality when Christ returns.

Five major warnings from God's Word are the following: do not be deceived by culture proclamations; believers will suffer persecution of some kind; be aware of false prophets; do not believe those who say *when* Christ will return; and avoid becoming overly occupied with the cares of the world.

Followers of Jesus (His sheep) hear His voice. He knows them and they follow Him.

For spiritual birth, we <u>a</u>dmit we are sinners, <u>b</u>elieve Jesus died for our sins, and <u>c</u>ommit our lives to Him. (ABC)

G-R-A-C-E is <u>G</u>od's <u>r</u>iches <u>a</u>t <u>C</u>hrist's <u>e</u>xpense.

In Christ, the gift of new life begins with each new day.

In this world you will have trouble. But take heart. I [Jesus] have overcome this world.

It is not too much to proclaim that Christ's resurrection is the most certain fact in all of history.

Jesus assures us that He is the truth and this truth sets us free.

Jesus came and said He will come again to give light to a dark world.

Jesus encourages people to distinguish between temporary and permanent matters.

Jesus has granted to the believer forgiveness, spiritual blessings, and salvation, and He has paid the debt to deliver us from this sinful world into the eternal world to come.

Jesus is the vine and we are the branches.

Jesus is the way, the truth and the life.

Jesus loves me, this I know, for the Bible tells me so.

Jesus makes us right with God through faith in Him.

Jesus paid a debt He did not owe because we owed a debt we could not pay.

Jesus promised that they who hear His Word and believe in Him who sent Him will have everlasting life, and they shall not come into condemnation but shall pass from death into life.

Jesus promises us that anyone who diligently sought Him would find Him.

Jesus' crucifixion assures each of us (all believers) of our salvation beyond doubt, instead of being forsaken because of our sinful nature.

Many people have trouble understanding the prosperity of the ungodly along with the suffering of the righteous. Why would a loving God seem to endorse such a system? The answer to this paradox is not apparent in the present time but in the world to come, where hell awaits the ungodly and heaven awaits those whom God has redeemed through faith in Christ. God's justice will prevail in His time.

No Jesus, no peace; know Jesus, know peace.

Nobody has dreamed up any moral advances since Christ's teachings.

Nothing comes close to positively impacting every aspect of life as Jesus.

One who drinks from the wells of the world will thirst again, but just a single drink from the springs of "living water" of which Christ spoke eliminates spiritual thirst forever.

Praise the Trinity: Father (God), Son (Jesus), and Holy Ghost (Spirit).

Something to strive for is less of us and more of Jesus.

The church is the community of believers who confess Jesus as Lord and Savior.

The goal of every believer is to conform to the image of Jesus.

The last promise in the Bible is that Jesus would return to earth again quickly. It seems evident that "quickly" must be understood in the sense of "suddenly."

The way of salvation is to believe in Jesus Christ as Lord and Savior.

The world needs to be prepared for the return of Jesus in person.

There are many paths one may follow in life, including the way of materialism and secularism; however, only one way leads to eternal life. Jesus said, "I am the way, the truth, and the life."

There is one God and one mediator (judge) between God and every human being, and that person (advocate) is Christ Jesus.

Those who believe in Jesus as their personal Savior will inherit eternal life in Heaven (present with God), and those who do not believe will inherit eternal life in Hell (absent from God).

Those who opt not to believe Christ will be granted their chosen status forever.

Unbelief in Christ is the only sin that God does not forgive.

We are all equal in Christ, Who by one Spirit has bonded us into one fellowship with Him and with one another, binding upon all people in every age.

We are all one (of equal value) in Christ Jesus.

We become disciples of Jesus when we learn and do the things He commands us to do to the best of our ability.

We must have a personal and active relationship with Jesus, our Savior.

We only love Jesus as much as the person we love the least.

What Jesus says and does are always perfect examples for us to follow.

When Jesus makes His second appearance, everything will be subjected to Him.

When Satan knocks, just send Christ to the door.

When we abide in Christ, His understanding fortifies us to face the issues of life.

When we focus on Christ, giving really feels good.

JOY

A life that reflects joy, praise, and thankfulness benefits everyone.

A prescription for joyful living includes something to hope for, something to do, and someone to love.

All are blessed when we express our joy.

At times our burdens can seem so heavy that the joy in our hearts is all but crushed.

Eliminate negative talk and introduce joy talk.

Face the future with joy and anticipation. God has great plans for each of us.

God promises that the more selflessly we give, the more we will receive joy.

It is foolish to deny ourselves joy by wishing we were in a future or past time.

Joy exists only in self-acceptance, not a perfect life.

Joy has its springs deep down inside; and those springs never, never run dry, no matter what happens.

Joy is an outward sign of inward faith in God's promises.

Joy is available to all who choose to put **J**esus first, **o**thers second, and **y**ourself third.

Positive emotions, such as contentment, gratitude, hope, joy, and love, enhance life beyond measure.

Seeking approval from others interferes with our potential for joy.

The words we mutter to ourselves have the power to encourage or discourage, to motivate or deflate, or to generate joy or deflate it.

To live a life of *maximum* joy, we must *minimize* the negative emotions that can dominate our life.

We would not invite a thief into our house, so why would we allow thoughts that steal our joy to make them at home in our house.

Weeping may linger for the night, but joy comes in the morning.

When we give up the need to be right, we expand our options and experience joy instead of stress.

JUDGMENT

People often make faulty judgments based on minimal information or hearsay.

People who judge others often do it to make themselves look better at the expense of others.

Such as every person is inwardly, so he or she judges outwardly.

We need to be more sensitive of others and not offend them, judge them, or cause them to stumble.

We were called to be witnesses, not lawyers or judges.

When we one day stand before our Creator, we will be judged by our obedience to Him, not our obedience to the secular world.

KINDNESS

A person with good character is accountable, caring, fair, honest, kind, sincere, trustworthy and more.

Be to other's virtues very kind; be to their faults, a little blind.

Before we say anything to anyone, ask this question: "Is it true, kind, or necessary?"

Blessings include a kindly nod, a special smile, and life itself upon the earth.

Compassionate (kind) actions involve working with ourselves as much as working with others.

If someone were to pay you two cents for every kind word you have spoken about people and five cents for every unkind word, would you be rich or poor?

Kind words are never wasted. Like scattered seeds, they spring up in unexpected places.

Kindness has converted more people than zeal, science or eloquence.

Kindness is the most desirable trait a person can have.

Life is made up of little things: smiles, kindnesses, obligations, and giving. They are what win and preserve the heart and generate comfort.

Meekness is the character of one who has the power to retaliate and yet remain kind – a vertical rather than horizontal attitude toward God.

Mercy (kindness) is what God grants to believers, even though they do not deserve it.

One of the greatest things we can do in this world is to be kind to someone.

Speak gently because people have enough they must endure without the addition of unkind words.

We are very smart if we are a little kinder and wiser than yesterday.

We must be active and earnest *in kindness*, not merely passive and inoffensive.

When we are filled with kindness and gentleness, there is no room for bitterness or self-centered motives. With God's help we can strive to speak gracious words that can strengthen families and communities by building people up, bridging gaps, and restoring broken relationships.

When we become discouraged and find it difficult to be kind and loving towards others, it helps to remember that God is supporting us.

Whoever is kind to the needy pleases and honors God because He wants what is best for everyone.

Without kindness, life is like a suitcase with no handle.

LIFE

A good life fears not life or death.

A lot of us feel threatened by the many mental and emotional giants that have evolved in our lives. Until these dragons are slain, peace of mind will evade us.

A rewarding life is about more than self. It means sharing with others.

After a reasonable time, it is best to let go of certain things in life.

All Scripture is inspired by God and is useful for teaching the truth, rebuking error, correcting faults, and giving instruction for right living, so that the person who serves God may be fully qualified and equipped to do every kind of good work.

Along the road of life, each one of us needs reliable direction for the journey.

Americans have the right to live as they please, as long as they are not interfering with the rights of other Americans to do the same.

Any permanent progress in life begins on the inside and spreads to the outside.

Because none of us have received a perfect upbringing, we have to learn to unlearn those things that do not make sense at this point in our lives and replace them with new learning; blaming keeps this from happening.

Before we can truly live in the present, we must let go of the past.

Believing in life after death makes a big difference on how one views dying.

Biblical principles are a blueprint for living; the proof is in the pudding.

Choose not to drop out of life.

Do not consider painful what improves life.

Each day we live is a priceless gift of God, loaded with possibilities to learn something new and to gain fresh insight.

Even a good thing can become a bad thing when it becomes a ruling force in our life.

Every aspect of our lives should be so ordered as to glorify God in whatever we think, say, and do.

Everyone is part of God's kingdom and each person is that special piece necessary to complete the puzzle called life.

For a more rewarding life, the challenge is to minimize the negative "stuff" and maximize the positive "stuff."

For many, life is what happens when not watching TV.

Give me the roses while I live, trying to cheer me on. Useless are the flowers that you give after I am gone.

Give people a fish and they eat for a day. Teach them to fish and they feed themselves for life.

Godly living involves our service to others via the use of our time, talents, abilities, and material possessions.

How much we get out of life is directly related to what we put into it as well as the lives of others.

If it is possible, as far as it depends on you, live at peace with everyone.

If we wish to live, we must first attend our funeral.

In order to live creatively and meaningfully, our self-concerns must be wedded to the concerns of others.

In the grand scheme of things, we have to learn to take whatever life brings and deal with it.

In this life, what we have, how we look, and what we can do dominate our existence. Externally, no part of *who* we are is more important than to whom we belong.

It is not what we gather but what we scatter that reflects what kind of lives we have lived.

It seems that a majority of people today ignore to whom they owe allegiance regarding life.

It takes many spokes to support the hub of the wheel of life, which allows it to turn and do its job.

Keeping life as simple as possible enables one to enjoy it more.

Letting the past totally dominate the present and future is contrary to sensible living.

Life can be hard by the yard, but by the inch, life is a cinch!

Life is a coin that we can spend any way we wish, but we can only spend it once.

Life is a gift, not a right, and our attitude should be one of thankfulness.

Life is constantly moving us in and out of "life-changing" places and relationships.

Life is filled with positive experiences that help us make it through the bad times. The ups and downs of life become clearer as we mature.

Life is like an onion: we peel it off one layer at a time.

Life is not a holiday but an education.

Life is not fair, but it is still a very precious gift.

Life is not passive activity. We are expected to sow, welcome, witness, and trust that even our smallest efforts could bear amazing fruit.

Life is short; enjoy it now!

Life is ten percent what happens to us and ninety percent how we respond to it.

Life is too short to waste time hating.

Life without boundaries is not all that it is cracked up to be. Just ask someone who has been there.

Live, almost, like you were dying. Everyone actually is.

Living in the moment reduces stress and helps us appreciate life more.

Living includes caring, crying, giving, growing, loving, sighing, and trying.

Living is like licking honey off a thorn.

Look around to see which violations of God's law are impacting humanity. How is your life affected by these violations?

Make the most of life now.

Meek people view themselves as sinners living among other sinners—no more, no less.

No one goes through life without suffering major disappointments; it is pain that often forces us to change.

Often understanding is a slow process that begins early in life and happens in such ways that we don't even realize we are learning.

Only after we look back on our lives, do we realize how much time, effort, and worry we devoted to things, situations, and circumstances that are out of our hands.

Our lives are as rivers, either useful in their energies or destructive in their force.

Our main mission in life is to be God's witnesses.

Our standards for living need to conform to God's Word.

People devoted to help make the world a better place are more inclined to see the brighter side of life.

People need a free conscience to discover what lifestyle is most meaningful for them.

Right thinking is the choice we have to make for ourselves for the rest of our life.

Self-centeredness complicates life; God-centeredness simplifies it.

Society tends to sway and change. God is our only constant in life.

Some of the secrets of a happy life are continuous, small treats.

Take hold of the stress in life or it will take hold of you.

Take the hard road so that life will be good.

The best things in life are not things.

The days and the years inevitably turn the pages and open a new chapter in our life.

The frailty and brevity of human life can be represented by the twin metaphors of withering grass and fading flowers, but the Word of God stands forever.

The greatest risk is the risk of "riskless" living.

The person who has the most to do with what happens to you in life is you!

The problems of life may distress our hearts, but the power of God is bigger than any storm we may encounter.

The right meditation will pave the way for a new life.

The soul, like the body, lives by what if feeds on.

The surest way to guarantee ourselves a miserable existence is to live only for self and not consider the good of others.

The way we live our lives is directly related to our established goals.

There is no greater freedom than living according to God's Word.

There is not one life flavor that suits every taste.

There is nothing so inevitable as changes in our lives.

Those who cannot endure the bad will not live to see the good.

Unrealistic expectations are the source of many of life's disappointments.

We (believers) look for the resurrection of the dead and life in the world to come. Amen.

We cannot live in tomorrows; we can only live in todays.

We do so many things in life that have no eternal value.

We have committed the Golden Rule to memory; let us now commit it to life.

We learn responsibility from our daily living.

We own the controlling voice in our lives.

We should focus on those things in life that will enhance our lives the most.

We should live our lives knowing that what we do is observed by others.

Whatever we hope to accomplish in life, we should do it as soon as possible.

When we are feeling overwhelmed by life's pressures, taking a hike (you name it) may be just the tonic we need for our troubled spirit.

When we change our focus, we change our life.

Wide is the gate and broad is the road that leads to destruction, and many enter through it; but small is the gate and narrow is the road that leads to life, and only a few find it.

Wisdom preserves the life of its possessor.

Without taking chances in life, one is always left to wonder about what could have been.

LOVE

A balanced life consists of faith, trust in God, kindness, and love of each other.

A humble heart complains less.

A merry heart does good like medicine.

Acceptance, encouragement and love help people become the person God wishes them to be.

After *love*, the most important word is *we*; the least important word is *I*.

All stand to benefit when we reach out with love to others.

All that truly matters in the end is that we loved.

As we think in our heart, so are we.

Be devoted to one another in brotherly love.

Becoming a better person is loving and being loved.

Behind all genuine good works, love will certainly surface.

Being a servant, among other things, includes teamwork, understanding, and an attitude of love.

Better to have loved and lost than never to have loved at all.

Caring is love in action. It is God at work in us.

Caring is the rock upon which love is built.

Cold, precise doctrine must never take away our love for people.

Even when all our physical needs are met, emotional desires, such as friendships, love, and hope, are great enhancements to life.

Every ass loves to hear himself bray.

Everyone that sincerely loves others is borne of God.

Everything good and loving has its source in God.

Faults are thick where love is thin.

God loves each one of us equally.

God loves us because of who God is, not because of what we are.

God's kind of love (agape) is unselfish, undeserved and unending.

God's love for us merits nothing less than total thanksgiving from us.

God's number one and two priorities: Spread the "Good News" of His love and care for those in need.

Heed not the worst in a person, but seek and love what is best in him or her.

How much we love God determines how much we love others and ourselves.

If you wish to be loved, love!

In the midst of our failures, God loves us and gives us the power to love others.

It is a pity and a shame how we break each other's hearts and cause each other pain.

It is better not to live than not to love.

It is better to talk less and love more.

It is easy to love the lovable.

It is much easier to pray for those we love than those not included in this group.

It is not how much we give, but how much love we put into it.

Keep our faces upturned to God as the flowers do to the sun. Look, and our souls shall love and grow.

Keeping a record is not love.

Kindness is a love guide that shows us how to live.

Knowledge takes a back seat to love.

Let us love not only in words, but also in deeds.

Let us not grow weary while doing good, for in due season we shall reap if we do not lose heart.

Live with no excuses and love with no regrets.

Love all, trust few, and do wrong to none.

Love cures people—the ones who receive it and the ones who give it.

Love draws people together. It does not separate.

Love erases offenses.

Love for others demonstrates God's presence in our lives.

Love has the awesome power to heal.

Love helps make trials bearable.

Love helps us mind and makes us kind to others every day.

Love is an event at which we give ourselves to other....

Love is essential. It is not an option.

Love is fulfilling God's law because He is Love.

Love is giving an outgoing concern for the welfare of others without expecting anything in return.

Love is not a demonstration. It is an inclination.

Love *is* patient, kind, helpful, trusting, and persevering. Love *is not* boastful, arrogant, envious, hateful, or resentful.

Love is spelled T-I-M-E.

Love is the universal language that is understood by all.

Love is why, when, where, and how much we give.

Love others just the way they are.

Love should be in the center of our being and in all that we do.

Love sought is good, but given unsought is better.

Loving our enemies does not mean thinking them to be nice, when it is quite plain they are not.

Most of us can do no great things—only small things with great love.

No eye has seen, nor ear heard, nor the human heart conceived what God has prepared for those who love Him.

No love is pure, so we all have to love in the midst of our own frailties and those of others.

No worse fate can befall a person in this world than to live and grow old alone, unloving, and unloved.

One believes with the heart and so is justified, and one confesses with the mouth and so is saved.

One forgives to the degree that one loves.

Opening our hearts helps us extend a genuine welcome to all we meet.

Our love for God comes from the heart.

Our three greatest needs are to be loved, to feel worthwhile, and to feel secure.

Performance love is not "real" love. It is "conditional" love.

Remember that the mind grows by what it takes in; the heart grows by what it gives out.

Say all the things that we want our loved ones to remember.

Scripture is not hard to understand, just hard to believe and even harder to obey. The secret is in the attitude of the heart with which one approaches it.

Sometimes we are called upon to speak the truth in love; however, we should do it with a spirit of gentleness, kindness and humility.

The actions of caring, giving, and sacrificing say "I love you."

The best way to reach others is to love them.

The good life is enhanced with the love, support, and affirmation of others.

The greatest healing agent in life is love.

The greatest thing in the world is LOVE.

The single most important word in any language is LOVE.

The two greatest commandments are "Love God" and "Love others."

There is only one kind of love, but there are a thousand imitations.

They that fall in love with themselves will have no rivals.

Those who deserve love the least need it the most.

To love our neighbors as ourselves is a truth for regulating society.

Trust in the Lord with all your heart and do not rely on your own insight.

Two things that help everybody are love and forgiveness.

Unless we are loved and can love others, emotional death is imminent.

Unselfish love (agape) sacrifices its own interests for the needs of others.

We express our love for God by how we treat other people.

We have the opportunity to demonstrate God's love to others in a way that no other person could ever do.

We love others because God first loved us.

We pardon to the degree that we love.

What we say at any given moment reveals the condition of our heats at that time.

When a person has no one to love him or her, suicide could seem to be the only option.

When the power of love overcomes the love for power, we will have peace.

Where your treasure is, there your heart will be also.

Without love, everyone is worse off.

Words of our mouths, thoughts of our hearts, and everything that we do must be filled with faith, hope, and love.

MORALS

As a society, we are moving in the direction of doing-away-with morality from our way of life. This has resulted in an increase of senseless acts of violence. Matters can only become worse with each succeeding generation.

Few, if anyone, would disagree that our moral values are disintegrating.

Freedom without moral commitment is aimless and promptly self-destructive.

God undertakes to ground us firmly in His truth and to protect us from moral and spiritual harm.

History proves that the loosening of moral bonds is the first stage of *disintegration*.

Immorality is "trending." The negative consequences are becoming more and more prevalent.

In these days of moral confusion with attitudes and actions once outlawed by society and now defended and favored, such as sexual promiscuity and others, there are great pressures on "God-believing" people to compromise their values with these non-Biblical desires.

Indifference may be legal, but it is immoral.

Materialism to extremes robs a nation of its moral values.

Moral values must be an active force in our way of life. We cannot prevent fires by simply buying more fire trucks.

Morality (rules of right and wrong) is indispensable to the maintenance of America; without it our country will collapse.

Morality in America, during the last few generations, continues on the road of decline. Many things contribute to the destructive behavior we are experiencing today. We are doing this with our thoughts, our words, and our actions. Conditions will only get worse until this trend is reversed.

No nation can remain free very long when immoral practices become widely accepted by a majority of its citizens.

Our nation is on a downward trend morally among children and young people with the reason being their parents and grandparents are following God's laws less.

Our sins (immoral behavior) hurt others and diminish us, and our lives bear the scars.

People need to maintain proven moral standards to make good choices.

Right moral choices produce positive results; wrong moral choices produce negative results.

The perspective regarding social morality has changed dramatically over the last generation or two. What was considered abnormal is now considered normal, such as promiscuous sex. We need to examine how these changes are impacting the whole of society.

There is a price to pay for rebellion and immoral behavior—negative consequences are guaranteed.

Those who choose a moral code of ethics grounded in Scripture will be well equipped to make all the right moral choices life will ever require.

To be carnally (immorally) minded is death, but to be spiritually minded is life with peace.

We are experiencing an immoral epidemic in America today.

We should not compromise our moral principles; let us be in the world but not of it.

We should resist allowing others to compromise our moral values.

We yearn for the person with self-control, temperance, and strong moral character.

Where morality is present, laws are almost unnecessary.

PATIENCE

God grant me patience, and I want it right now!

Patience is a form of action.

Patience is a skill we can learn.

Patience is never obtained through bored indifference.

Patience is the companion of wisdom.

We can all benefit from God's patience.

PRAYER

A sinning person will stop praying; a praying person will stop sinning.

Do not pray when it is "raining," if you do not pray when it is "sunny."

Expect four out of five traffic lights to be red; devote waiting time to introspection and prayer.

God speaks to us through His Word as recorded in the Bible, worship, and prayer.

If Christians spent as much time praying as they do grumbling, they would soon have nothing to grumble about.

In prayer, it is better to have a heart without words than words without heart.

It is not well for a person to pray cream and live skim milk.

Our prayers are not in vain even when the results are not what we expected.

Prayer is not designed to change God; it is to change us.

Prayer is the key to heaven, but faith unlocks the door.

Praying for people who treat us with contempt is one way to do good to those who hate us.

PUSH: Pray until something happens.

The prayer that says it all is "Thank you."

There is no time that is not a good time for prayer.

We do well to pray and not lose heart, then trust and wait on God.

We should pray fewer prayers of "please" and more prayers of "thank you."

RELATIONSHIPS

A relationship is a two-way street.

An affair is thought to be the most insurmountable problem in a marriage.

An increase in cheating reflects deep anxiety and insecurity in America nowadays, desperation even, as well as arrogance among the rich and cynicism among ordinary people.

As our relationship with God is holy, relationships between husbands and wives should be sacredly guarded.

Avoid any person or relationship that would slowly prod you down the wrong path.

Blessed are the husband and wife who are as polite and courteous to one another as they are to their friends.

Divorce can be more devastating to family members than death.

Everyone has a degree of narcissism (self-preoccupation); however, it becomes a problem when one or both partners are unable to empathize with and support the other.

Feed the marriage relationship with patience, kindness, and reasonableness.

For a marriage to be peaceful, the husband should be deaf and the wife blind.

Giving thanks helps us feel closer in our relationships and increases our happiness.

Healthy relationships require clear boundaries.

If a relationship has to be a secret, we should not be in it.

Intimacy is the ability to let ourselves be known.

It takes both partners for their marriage to thrive; each is responsible for enhancing it.

It takes time and effort to build healthy relationships.

Just one praiseworthy statement about a person can save a relationship.

Many men spell love S-E-X; women spell it R-E-L-A-T-I-O-N-S-H-I-P.

Many people are lonely because they build walls instead of bridges in their relationships.

Marriage and family are two of the greatest blessings one could possibly experience.

Marriage is the most challenging decision two people will ever make in life.

Marriage, at its best, is when each partner gives as close to one hundred percent as possible and puts the other one's needs before his or her own.

Once we realize we do not have to make ourselves wrong to deliver an apology, we will experience a new power.

Our relationships are best carried out by submitting to one another in reverence to God.

Relationships have a good chance of improving when both partners are willing to look at themselves and make some adjustments or changes.

Relationships thrive with caring, encouragement, and praise.

The four prerequisites for unity are humility, love, spirit, and mercy.

The key to a good marriage is having two good forgivers.

True love always has joys and sorrows.

When a wife or husband sins, neither one is totally innocent.

When we give little to a relationship, we should not expect much in return.

When you marry, you marry his or her family members as well.

SIN

Any use of sex except as an expression of love and procreation in marriage is sinful and breaks the Seventh Commandment.

Being helpless, ungodly, sinful, and God's enemy does not make one ineligible to receive God's grace.

Christ died for us while we were yet sinners and that proves God's love for us.

Confession is what believers do when they sin.

Either the Bible will keep you away from sin or sin will keep you away from the Bible.

God does not hold our sinful past against us if we place our trust in Him.

God is the one who defines sin (disobeying His Word). He will make the ultimate judgment.

God's Word is true. People do not realize that sin (wrong behavior) always destroys.

Great crimes never come singly; they are linked to sins that went before.

If we are honest, we have to admit that sin finds its place in the lives of all of us.

No amount of sin in our lives prevents God's acceptance of us.

No matter how many new translations of the Bible come out, we still sin in the same way.

Our sins will be remembered against us no more, if we have been eternally redeemed.

Repentance (changed minds) is what sinners (which include everyone) do before they become believers.

Repentance is a change of mind and direction and a turning away from sin.

Salvation is our greatest need because we are all born with a sinful nature and, therefore, need a Savior.

Showing favoritism with people on any basis is a sinful act.

Sin (evil) has diminished the value of human life, but God's love deems it priceless.

Sin (wrong actions) always has negative consequences—guaranteed.

Sin (wrong) destroys our will power. It saps our will to live righteously (right).

Sin destroys willpower. It saps our strength to live righteously.

Sin is an offense against God's laws. Traditionally, the original Seven Deadly Sins are pride, covetousness, lust, anger, gluttony, envy, and sloth.

Sin sees the bait but is blind to the hook.

Sinning destroys much good.

The Bible states that we are to refrain from "sin" as God defines it, and that in so doing, we will benefit others as well as ourselves.

The closer one gets to God, the more clearly one sees his or her sinfulness and the more wonderful becomes His amazing grace.

The more sins (wrongs) committed, the more locked doors, the more crimes, the more jails and prisons.

The sin of pride (arrogance) was the very first sin and is still the most difficult sin to overcome.

The sins people commit two-by-two must be paid for one-by-one.

The terrible result of being enslaved to sin is that it will destroy us.

The worst bondage of all is slavery to sin.

There is not one person on this earth who is without sin.

Though we sin, God does not withhold His mercy, pardon, and love.

We are all slaves to sin.

We are captives of sin (vice), and the only way to free ourselves is by faith and trust in God.

We are not punished *for* our sins, but *by* them.

We do well to confess rather than conceal our sins; God knows what they are. Then, we should repent and try not to repeat them.

We must at least be as concerned to correct wrong (sin) in ourselves as we are in others.

SPIRITUALITY

All of us are faced with a second spiritual birth. It is a gradual unfolding process that continues throughout life depending on what each person chooses: either God-centered or self-centered.

Choosing to live a Godly life is what the Bible refers to as one's second (spiritual) birth; this new life will be demonstrated by one's love and concern for others.

Confusion results when people resort to worldly rather than Godly wisdom to resolve spiritual matters.

Life is a four-sided affair: physical, mental, social and spiritual. It is a four-fold opportunity to grow. It helps us to touch life at all angles, absorb strength from all contacts, and pour out power on all fronts. The more we pour out, the more we find to pour.

Nurture strength of spirit to shield us in sudden misfortunes.

Our spiritual house (our heart) suffers when left unattended.

The Bible teaches of physical birth over which we have no choice and spiritual birth over which we have total choice.

The life-giving Word of God returns to Him, not void, but full of the spiritual fruit for which He sent it.

The Word of God is the basic spiritual food He provides to His "children."

Unavoidable priorities are spiritual, family, neighbors, health, work, education, money and material comfort.

We are not human beings having a spiritual experience; we are spiritual beings having a human experience.

When we live according to our own moral standards, we might feel good about ourselves, but that doesn't make us spiritually healthy.

TOLERANCE

A mature person thinks twice before offending someone over a personal issue.

A person is rich according to what he or she is, not according to what he or she has.

Accept me as I am, then I can change.

Accepting others in a nonjudgmental way does not mean agreeing with them.

Accountability is applicable to everyone because we reap what we sow.

Affirmation brings out the best in people.

Attitude can make the difference between acceptance and rejection.

Avoid "picky" word fights started by quarrelsome individuals.

Avoid blaming because it makes matters worse; rather, explore solutions.

Be respectful of differences among people.

Being different is not easy; it is one reason that conformity is so popular.

Do not stand up for a bad cause.

Don't compare yourself to others. You have no idea what their journey is all about.

Don't judge each day by the harvest you reap but by the seeds you plant.

Each person should have a formula that defines his or her limitations.

Envy is a waste of time. We already have all we need.

Everybody is ignorant, only on different subjects.

Everyone should be quick to listen, slow to speak, and slow to become angry.

Giving advice is best received when people request it.

God is the source of everything that makes men, men and women, women. They differ physically, mentally, and emotionally, but they are complementarily equal.

Heed not the worst in a person, but seek and love what is best in him or her.

However good or bad a situation is, it will change.

If we all threw our problems in a pile and saw everyone else's, we would grab ours back.

If we want to change the way we live, we must change the way we think.

If we would try our best to see life from the other person's viewpoint, we would be more humane and empathetic.

In matters of principle, stand like a rock; in matters of taste, swim with the current.

In one minute, hour, day, month or year(s), will this matter?

It doesn't take all kinds; there just happen to be all kinds.

It is better not to prejudge people. The ground at the cross is level.

It is error only and not truth that shrinks from inquiry.

It is not what other people think of us, it is what we think of ourselves.

Making fun of people never helps and always hurts.

More people are making their own rules, setting their own standards, and living their own way. This can and in many ways will only end in disaster.

Negative feelings "stuffed" alive never die.

Nobody can please everybody all of the time.

None knows the weight of another's burden.

Not being known does not stop the truth from being truth.

Often the very traits that most annoy us in others are ones we possess.

Other people's business is usually not our business.

People are born equal, but they are also born different.

People do not change by being put down; they change by being lifted up.

Rather than cling to certain old ways, we need to embrace the new.

Some cause happiness wherever they go; others whenever they go.

The people to be most pitied are those who maintain closed minds.

This, too, shall pass away.

Tolerating what is destructive (wrong) does not make it constructive (right).

Truth will always be truth, regardless of lack of understanding, disbelief or ignorance.

Unique characteristics of gender do not make one superior over the other.

United we stand, divided we fall.

Vanquish an angry person by gentleness.

We live in a dishonest (cheating) culture, unfortunately.

We must do everything possible to focus on the many positive aspects around us.

We must have a willingness to care deeply about divided groups, and a commitment to work for and with each party.

We must learn to unlearn and then relearn.

We must meet one another doing good.

We need to practice daily the art of affirming and supporting others.

We should not be conformed to this world but be transformed by the renewing (renovating) of our minds, so that we may discern what is the will of God, what is good, acceptable, and perfect.

We tend not to see things as *they* are, but as *we* are.

What cannot be altered must be borne, not blamed.

When we help bear someone's burden, we will fulfill God's plan for us.

TRUTH

A danger foreseen is half avoided.

A difficult past can be overcome by continuing to move on.

A frog tried to look as big as an elephant and burst.

A gentle answer turns away wrath, but a harsh word stirs up anger.

A just cause is not ruined by a few mistakes.

A little lie is like a little pregnancy; it does not take long before everybody knows.

A man there was and they called him mad; the more he gave, the more he had.

A mind that is disciplined and purified is ready for victorious actions.

A person who can laugh at himself or herself will never cease to be amused.

A river becomes crooked by following the line of least resistance. So do people.

A small group of thoughtful, committed citizens can change the world; it is the only thing that ever has.

A smile is an inexpensive way to improve one's looks.

A thousand curses hurt but never tore a shirt.

A train is free to travel only when it remains on the tracks.

Acceptance and tolerance do not necessarily imply agreement and/or approval.

According to a doctor, there are no drugs that are one hundred percent safe; however, there are occasions when their use is the lesser of two evils.

Acknowledging our mistakes helps keep us humble.

Act as if what you do makes a difference. It does.

After establishing the right priorities, we must maintain our focus on each of those priorities.

All kids are gifted; some just open their packages earlier than others.

All of our choices produce some kind of consequences.

All of us are expected to be a servant in one capacity or another.

All of us have good in us, just as we all have bad.

All of us should have the equal opportunity to develop our talents.

All stand to benefit when we are grounded and rooted in truth.

All will experience anger, despair, and hurt.

All wrongs will be righted and truth will come to light.

Almost everyone has his or her version of what is fair. The question remains, "Who is right?"

Although feelings fluctuate, consequences last forever.

Although I may not walk with kings, let me be big in little things.

Always do your best. What you plant now, you will harvest later.

An ant on the move does more than a dozing ox.

An eye for an eye makes the whole world blind.

Anything worth doing is worth doing well.

As far as possible, without surrender, be on good terms with all people.

As relentlessly as we may try, we cannot think one thing and experience something else.

At the core of "posing" (lack of purity) lies hypocrisy.

Authority comes not by telling others what to do, but from doing the things you want others to do.

Avoid looking backward or forward and try to keep looking upward.

Bad officials are elected by good citizens who do not vote.

Be aware of solicitors (telemarketers); they usually have a hidden agenda.

Be courageous about doing what is right and take responsibility for your actions.

Be the change you want to see in the world.

Be what you are. This is the first step toward becoming better than you are.

Be willing to compromise but never compromise your principles.

Because of our "fallen nature," we are all born with weaknesses and tendencies to evil and need to be redeemed.

Because we have a "skinny" belly doesn't mean we don't have a "fat" head.

Because yesterday is a cancelled check and tomorrow is a promissory note, we must spend today's "cash" wisely.

Becoming more optimistic takes time, effort, and determination; but it can be done.

Being a slave to the opinions of others makes for a less than desirable existence.

Being in the majority can get us into a lot of trouble.

Being mean to others might make us feel good for a while, but it is bad for all in the end.

Better to ask twice than lose your way once.

Biblical truth protects us from false worship.

Big mouthfuls often choke the swallower.

Blamers point the finger at someone else or thing for their own problems. It is so popular because it temporarily liberates them but does not get to the root of the problem.

Brighten the corner where you are.

Celebrate every day, not just holidays, because every day is special.

Change is inevitable.

Change occurs from the bottom up. It takes concerned, inspired, and dedicated individuals to make it happen.

Choose to be the statue or the bird.

Comfort has never enriched the world as much as adversity has.

Common sense is not so common.

Common sense tells us nothing is free.

Communication evolves in more ways than words. Consider the following: a smile, a greeting, a thought, or a helpful deed.

Communication is hearing what has not been said.

Complete the most important things first; it is usually the best course of action.

Conscience is the compass of the soul.

Convert challenging situations into learning opportunities.

Death is the beginning and not the end of our journey.

Democracy only guarantees equal opportunity, not conditions.

Do not be envious of evil people who prosper materially. Their day of reckoning will come.

Do not be overcome by evil but overcome evil with good.

Do not be squeezed into the mold of the world's culture.

Do not evaluate each day by the harvest you reap, but by the seeds you plant.

Do not take revenge.

Do not talk unless it improves the silence.

Do not use harmful words in talking. Use only helpful words, the kinds that build up and provide what is needed, so that what you say will do good to those who hear you.

Do the next best thing.

Dwelling on our problems doesn't fix them; it just makes us experts on them.

Each day begins with this thought: "Today" is the beginning of the rest of my life.

Each of us has a calling. We are invited to use our gifts to serve others and spread the good news.

Each of us is expected to be a servant in one capacity or another.

Each person should use whatever gift he or she has received to serve others.

Enforcing the laws already in the book should happen before new laws are made.

Enjoy the peace of a clear conscience.

Essentials should not take a back seat to incidentals.

Evening news is where they begin with "Good evening" and then proceed to tell you why it is not.

Every generation seems to have to cope with its own unique set of problems and challenges.

Every great achievement was once considered impossible.

Every path has its puddle.

Every right implies responsibility, every opportunity an obligation, and every possession a duty.

Every vice has its excuse ready.

Everybody eventually surrenders to something or someone.

Everyone has to think to be polite; the first impulse is to be impolite.

Everyone we will ever meet knows something we don't.

Everything is permissible, but not everything is beneficial.

Everything that we see, hear, feel, or think influences how we perceive what is right and what is wrong. Since all of us have learned wrong things, we need to learn to unlearn and relearn. We can do this by filtering everything through God's truth word.

Fill up the crevices of time with the things that matter most.

Flattery usually has strings attached.

Focus on the solution to the matter; refuse to play the "blame game."

Freedom is never license to do as we please, but only to do as we ought.

Freedom is not procured by a full enjoyment of what is desired, but by controlling the desire.

Genius is one percent inspiration and ninety-nine percent perspiration.

God is light (truth) and in Him is no darkness (lies).

God of the Bible is all in all: truth, righteousness, peace, love, patience, comfort, hope, grace, glory, and salvation.

God's attitude towards individuals is determined by their love of truth rather than knowledge of the truth.

God's recorded Word is the truth and it is the same "yesterday, today, and tomorrow."

God's truth often comes in ways people choose not to accept.

Habits are generally too small to be felt until they are too strong to be broken.

Happiness is a state of mind that depends entirely on the individual involved.

He who builds to every man's advice will have a crooked house.

Helping those who refuse to work only makes matters worse.

History is filled with great civilizations that have come and gone. They all experienced more decay from within.

Honor and a good name are easily taken away but not easily restored.

Houseguests are like fish; they begin to smell after three days.

Humility is making the most of what we do not like.

Humility is not thinking less of yourself; it is thinking of yourself less.

Humility is to make a right estimate of one's self.

Hurting others and being hurt by them is a two-way street.

I grumbled because I had no shoes until I met a person who had no feet.

I would agree with you, but then we would both be wrong!

I would rather one walk with me than merely tell the way.

Ideas are a dime a dozen. People who put them into action are priceless.

If our minds are not mostly at ease, our bodies become diseased.

If painful recollections of the past or frightening thoughts of the future come to mind, we can put them away.

If people were angels no laws would be necessary.

If the wind will not serve, take to the oars.

If uncertain about your priorities, talk to someone who has an incurable disease.

If we are looking for trouble, we will soon find it.

If we are not fit to face death today, it is very unlikely we will be by tomorrow.

If we can change our situation, we should do it; if we cannot change it, then we should change ourselves.

If we compare ourselves with others, we could become vain and bitter—not a good thing to do.

If we don't bloom where we are, chances are we will not bloom at all.

If we fail to plan, we plan to fail.

If we have tender thoughts about people, we should tell them now.

If we keep thinking of ourselves the way we used to be, that is exactly what we will continue to be.

If we think something is mean and hurtful, think how the person on the receiving end feels.

If we want people to trust us, do not give them reason not to.

If you cannot catch a bird of paradise, better take a wet hen.

If you do a favor, forget it; if you receive one, remember it.

If you do not crack the shell, you cannot eat the nut.

If you don't ask, you don't get.

If you don't know where you are going, any road will get you there.

If you really want insight about yourself, ask someone you know, trust, and respect.

If you run after two hares, you will catch neither.

If you wait until you are really sure, you will never take off the training wheels.

If you want to remember to take something with you, place your car keys there.

In heaven, there are no tears.

In the eyes of the blind, the one-eyed man is king.

In the near future certain people are going to begin asking themselves, "Whatever possessed me to get tattooed?"

Indeed, there is much in the world about which to "greatly rejoice."

Individuals are mortal, but truth is immortal.

It has been said that the only easy way to deal with change is when we are the ones wishing to change.

It is a good thing when other people are made to feel welcomed.

It is all right to sit on your pity pot every now and then. Just be sure to flush when done.

It is better not to vow than to make a vow and not fulfill it.

It is better to be alone than remain in the presence of bad company.

It is easier to prepare and prevent than to repair and repent.

It is easier to ridicule than to commend.

It is far easier to be pulled down than lifted up.

It is hard to be silent when we have nothing to say.

It is impossible to control and change others. We have our hands full controlling and changing ourselves.

It is much easier to blame than to face up to our responsibilities.

It is not always what happens to us that can be so devastating, but how we view it.

It is not easy to understand what people might become.

It is not what goes into our mouth that defiles us, but what comes out.

It is so easy to say what we would do, as opposed to what another person did.

It is well to drop the old so that one may seize the new.

It is your point of view that decides what you see.

It takes courage and perseverance to bring about change.

It takes two to cause a quarrel.

It would be a good thing if we expended energy on teaching people not to be offended when someone offers a different opinion, because we can learn something from everybody.

Just as the twig is bent, the tree is inclined.

Just do something for someone else when you have the opportunity.

Know how to refuse.

Know your chief asset, cultivate it, and help along others.

Laughter is the closest distance between two people.

Learn to appreciate what you have before time makes you appreciate what you had.

Learn to paddle your own canoe.

Learning is discovering that something is possible.

Lesser minds have a talent of talking much and saying little.

Let every year make us a better person.

Let go of those expectations created by what society demands.

Let go of what we cannot keep or alter.

Let no one ever come to you without leaving better and happier.

Let not the sun go down upon your anger.

Let us be true to our obligations.

Let your past be your springboard, not your quicksand.

Liars will not be believed, even when they speak the truth.

Lies (darkness) oppose the revelation of truths (light).

Like a gold ring in a pig's snout is a beautiful woman who shows no discretion.

Long explanations tend to lead to disappointing endings.

Long-term results should be considered before deciding on a course of action.

Lose yourself in serving others.

Make your point and then stop. Don't beat a dead horse.

Manners can vex, soothe, corrupt, purify, exalt, debase, barbarize, or refine us.

Many of us crucify ourselves between two thieves: regret for the past and fear for the future.

Many people are influenced more by the surrounding culture than the truth.

Many people overvalue what they are not and undervalue what they are.

Maturity is the ability to bear an injustice without wanting to get even.

Meekness is the opposite of weakness.

Meekness often means to go against the flow.

Men—their rights and nothing more; women—their rights and nothing less.

Minds are like parachutes; they only function when open.

Minimize looking back and looking forward and maximize the present.

More learning can evolve from mourning than rejoicing.

More things have been gained by knack than by knock.

Most of the choices we make require waiting.

Most of the greatest good in the world has been done by the fewest people.

Most of us are better talkers than listeners.

Most of us are blind to our faults.

Most of us do not aim too high and miss. We aim too low and hit.

Most of us trip over the small stuff.

Most of what we worry about never comes to pass, but most of us still worry.

Most people are unaware of the connection between their state of mind and their circumstances that eventually causes them to settle for far less than their God-given best.

Most people know more about what makes others tick, than they know about themselves.

Never grow so old that you cannot change your mind.

Never wrestle with a pig. You both get all dirty and the pig likes it.

No matter what we say, it is our actions that speak for us.

No one is a fool always; everyone is sometimes.

No one is an island.

No one is defeated until he or she starts blaming someone else.

No person is so tall that he need never stretch and none so small that he need never stoop.

No temptation has seized us except what is common to all.

No work, however humble, dishonors a person.

Nobody ever outgrows Scripture; the book widens and deepens with our years.

None but ourselves can free our minds.

Not all disabilities are physical or visible. It doesn't hurt to assume that everyone is hurting in one way or another.

Nothing comes to the person who just waits.

Nothing is to be had for nothing.

Nothing is troublesome that we do willingly.

Obedience acknowledges that we serve a higher power than ourselves. At times, we do not ask for guidance because we think that we know the answer.

Of all the things we wear, our expression makes the greatest impact.

Of making and reading many books there is no end, and much study wearies the body.

Old age eventually comes to everyone who survives youth and middle age, but that does not mean it is time to quit.

One lie spoils a thousand truths.

One thing we can't recycle is time, so we shouldn't waste it.

One's happiness is one's own responsibility.

Opportunity does not even need to knock if you leave your door open.

Opportunity may knock once, but temptation bangs on your front door forever.

Our actions should attract rather than drive others away.

Our culture has abandoned the gold standard, moving from gold to silver, to bronze, to iron, to clay, and to mud.

Our expressed words are either helpful or harmful; seldom, if ever, are they neither.

Our gracious God is the God of comfort, grace, joy, love, mercies, peace, and truth.

Our thoughts are triggered by our surroundings, our memories, and our imagination.

Our words should not be crude, obscene, foolish, bitter, false, or malicious; instead, they should be good, true, and gracious, so that they build up those who hear them.

Our YES should mean YES and our NO should mean NO.

Patient people make the most of trying times and circumstances.

Pay off your credit card(s) every month.

People are all alike in their promise. It is only in their deed that they differ.

People are much more important than things.

People are not necessarily against us, they are merely for themselves.

People can be very discouraging if we allow them to be so.

People can generally find a way to do what they want to do, and they can find a hundred excuses for what they do not want to do.

People grow from their weaknesses, not their strengths.

People need more to be reminded than to be instructed.

People spend up to a third more when paying with credit instead of cash.

People usually do their best in the situation they find themselves.

People usually do what they do to survive and are unlikely to expend extra effort when it is necessary.

People want to know how much we care, not how much we know.

People who choose not to obey the law must prepare to live with the consequences.

People who drift to the far right or far left usually end up in the ditch.

People who have little and want less are happier than those who have much and want more.

Perseverance is the key to escape and personal satisfaction.

Personal circumstances must be resolved to the best of our ability because we cannot run away from them.

Pick up a grain a day and add to your heap.

Please all and you will please none.

Pour not water on a drowning mouse.

Power tends to corrupt and absolute power corrupts absolutely.

Pride builds walls between people; humility builds bridges.

Pride is the only disease known to man that makes everyone sick except the one who has it.

Progress is made one step at a time.

Quality should have priority over quantity.

Quarrels are quickly settled when deserted by one party.

Quarrels, more often than not, start over petty, unimportant matters.

Rather than expect perfection, settle for daily improvement.

Rejoice with those who rejoice; mourn with those who mourn.

Remember mistakes just long enough to profit by them.

Resentment diminishes and devours the self.

Responsible people do not elevate their interests above others' needs by taking advantage of them.

Right thoughts will generate right actions.

Routine lies at the heart of discipline.

Run away from untested and deceitful desires.

Salvation will bring about good works.

Self-centered people can ignore the wisdom of the ages but not the consequences.

Set our minds on things above, not earthly.

Since all husbands and wives are far from perfect, they should not expect perfection in each other.

Since we are like no other human being ever created since the beginning of time, we are incomparable.

Some people may possibly entertain angels without knowing it.

Sometimes you have to go really high to understand how small you really are.

Stand firm in what is right in the face of all kinds of opposition.

Statistics are like a bikini: what they reveal is suggestive, but what they conceal is vital.

Strive to be what you wish to be thought to be.

Suffering will come to everyone.

Suppressed anger is often at the root of depression.

Talk only about what is true, honest, just, pure, lovely, and of good reports.

Talkers are no good doers.

Teachers affect eternity; they can never tell where their influence stops.

The "put-down" runs pretty deep and stays with us a long, long time.

The best contraception is the word NO repeated frequently.

The clergy's main function is to teach and equip people to "minister" to other people.

The crying cat catches nothing.

The driving population needs to be more serious regarding distractions while driving, such as texting. They need to understand the risks to themselves and other people.

The future is only a dream and the past no longer exists. The present moment is the only reality.

The greatest legacy we can leave to the next generation is a spiritual one – God's truth.

The less people know, the more they think they know; the more people know, the less they think they know.

The longer the explanation, the greater the possibility the person is trying to conceal the truth.

The longer we wait, the closer we get to receive promises.

The more one has, the more one worries.

The more we seek to become satisfied as consumers, the emptier we can become.

The only journey is the journey within.

The only people without problems are those in cemeteries.

The second vice is lying; the first is running into debt.

The sensible thing to do is to celebrate what we presently have.

The smallest good deed is better than the greatest intention.

The sort of thing we say is the thing that will be said to us.

The time is always right to do what is right.

There are better things ahead than any we leave behind.

There are some things that cannot be learned in books but only by experience, and obedience is surely one of those things.

There are two kinds of complainers: men and women.

There is a time for everything and a season for every activity under heaven.

There is hardly anybody good for everything, and there is scarcely anybody who is absolutely good for nothing.

There is more that unites than divides us. Why not focus on the former rather than the latter?

There is no delight in owning anything unshared.

There is no happiness in having, or in getting, or in being served, but only in giving and serving others.

There is no pillow so soft as a clear conscience.

There is nothing hidden that will not be disclosed, and nothing concealed that will not be known or brought out in the open.

There is nothing permanent except change.

There probably is no other truth in the Bible hated more by unbelievers than that of everlasting punishment.

There will always be something new and exciting: new insights, understanding, and people to meet.

Think how happy we would be if we lost everything we have right now—and then got it back again.

Think not of others' faults; look for what is good.

Thinking is not agreeing or disagreeing. That is voting.

This too shall pass away.

Those that fear not the future may enjoy the present.

Those who are much occupied with the appearance of the body, usually give little thought to the care of the soul.

Those who lack self-confidence usually overreact to constructive criticism.

Those who want to do a great deal of good at once seldom do anything.

To improve is to change; to approach perfection is to change often.

To what we devote our attention will be elevated in our consciousness.

Treat people as they are and they will remain that way. Treat them as they could be and they may become as they could be.

True Christian faith means to be completely persuaded that there is no other truth apart from the Word of God on which we might build our life.

Truth and oil always rise to the surface.

Truth can be viewed in three ways: my truth, your truth, and THE truth (God's).

Truth has never been popular with the masses.

Truth is absolute or it is not truth.

Truth is what stands the test of experience.

Try treating everyone (spouse included) as if he or she is your "customer."

Trying to drink eight glasses of water a day could be detrimental to one's mental health.

Two ears and one mouth could remind us to listen twice as much as we speak.

Two people must eat a bushel of salt together before they really know each other.

Unless we can identify with some sort of loyalty, we will not find unity and peace in our active living.

Use what we have. Start doing it. Expect it to happen. (USE)

Usually secular truth is somewhere between the two extremes.

Vision without action is a daydream; action without vision is a nightmare.

Waste can be minimized by using it up, making it do, wearing it out, and doing without.

We all must guard against culture pollution.

We all struggle with hypocrisy, saying one thing and meaning another.

We all, like sheep, have gone astray, each of us turning to his or her own way.

We are born with tendencies toward both good and evil.

We are created in the image of the Master Creator.

We are meant to lean on each other.

We are never too old to learn something stupid.

We are not defined by what happens to us, but by how we respond to what happens to us.

We are not made for a time; we are made for eternity.

We are responsible for our actions and reactions regarding any matter.

We are to bloom where we have been planted and not yield to the restless desire for change.

We are to speak our truth quietly and clearly and listen to others, even the dull and the ignorant. They, too, have their story.

We are what we repeatedly do.

We are who we allow ourselves to become.

We become what we are committed to.

We can all sense a mysterious connection to each other; therefore, it makes sense to practice "The Golden Rule."

We can and should choose how we respond to circumstances.

We can avoid reality, but we cannot avoid the consequences of avoiding reality.

We can grow, learn, and trust just as much or more presently than we ever did in the past.

We can lose the reality of the forest because we are looking too closely at each tree.

We can move a ton of bricks, a few at a time.

We can only make a first impression once!

We cannot run with the hare and hunt with the hounds.

We do not need to solve all the problems we encounter. We just need to try.

We do not remember days, we remember moments. Make moments worth remembering.

We give people permission to make us angry.

We have to move forward to have a chance to experience the victory.

We help people the most by loving them and challenging them to be all they can be.

We must be strong and carry on.

We must determine our calling in order to know which road to travel.

We must guard against letting our roots get down too deep in our materialistic world.

We must like what we have when we do not have what we like.

We must not let our expectations and obligations pile up beyond our capacity.

We must nurture great thoughts, for we will never go higher than our thoughts.

We need to see the glass as half full and not half empty.

We need to think about, ask questions about, and take responsibility for our actions.

We often are so busy seeing through other people that we have little or no time, inclination, or desire to see them through.

We often let our fear of making a mistake keep us from enjoying the pleasure of serving.

We rarely think about the things we think about.

We seldom reflect how pleasant it is to ask for nothing.

We should correct those things we can and accept those things we cannot correct.

We should go after what we will take with us when we die.

We should look for the best in people and bring it to their attention.

We should make every effort to do what we have to do when it ought to be done whether we like it or not.

We should not allow other people or things to determine our frame of mind. Each person is personally responsible for this.

We suffer more from imagination than from reality.

We usually reproduce what we come from.

We will help others more by focusing on their strengths instead of their weaknesses.

We, the people, must promote removing the changes in our culture that are destructive and replacing them with those that are constructive.

Wealth often enlarges rather than satisfies appetite.

What comes out of our mouths is a reflection of our inner thoughts.

What people do has much more of an impact than what they say.

What we dwell on becomes increasingly prominent in our minds and determines our actions.

What we want or expect to see colors what we actually see.

Whatever people are sowing, this they will also reap.

Whatever we dwell upon becomes prominent in our minds.

Whatever we have, we must either use or lose.

Whatever your hands find to do, do it with all of your might.

When faced with a challenge, young people can learn to make good decisions by asking themselves: "What kind of person do I want to be?"

When people "resist the truth," they will "believe a lie."

When people acquire knowledge, they become the ultimate beneficiaries.

When people begin to exhibit distain for God's truth, there may soon come a time in their lives when they find it impossible to believe in the Creator.

When people follow God's truth, there is no limit to the blessings that they may receive, such as love, joy, peace, patience, kindness, goodness, faithfulness, gentleness, and self-control.

When people with different values "hang out" together, somebody ultimately changes.

When we accept responsibility for our weaknesses, we are less likely to blame and criticize other people.

When we do our own thing, our own thing does us.

When we practice compassion, we detach ourselves from the situation and do not over-personalize it.

When we see ourselves as we "really" are, we tend to be more tolerant of others.

When we walk with a cripple, we learn to limp.

When you are not sure which course of action to take regarding others, put yourself in their place.

When you cannot get a compliment in any other way, pay yourself one.

Where real repentance is present, there is obedience.

Where we have been, what we have done, and where we are now matters far less than where we are headed.

Wherever we go, we take ourselves with us.

Whoever digs a pit often ends up in it.

With all its sham, drudgery, and broken dreams, the world is still a beautiful place.

Worry is like a rocking chair: it gives you something to do but never gets you anywhere.

Xenocrates, a pupil of Plato, had it right when he said he had often regretted his speaking but never his silence.

Yelling louder does not make a weak point strong.

You are only young once, but you can be immature forever.

You cannot unscramble eggs.

You never will know the worth of water until the well is dry.

VIRTUES

Gratitude is not only the greatest of virtues, but also it is the parent of all other virtues.

Humility is an attitude of mind.

Humility is the foundation of all other virtues.

If we are to use sex in the way God created us, we must restrict it to the marriage relationship and not to our thoughts, wishes, and desires.

It is more blessed to give than to receive, one of the least practiced virtues in the Bible.

Love is the highest virtue.

Meekness says that God is always right.

Nothing is of more importance for the public welfare than to form and train up youth in wisdom and virtue.

One of the highest expectations we can have of one another is forgiveness.

Pious actions can become sinful when they spring from impure motivation.

Race, color and gender should not be factors in how we view people.

Self-control is required in our spiritual lives if we are to take in only what is nourishing and uplifting.

Sexual purity and resisting both fornication and adultery (Seventh Commandment) enhances the marriage relationship.

Temperance is moderation in things that are good and total abstinence from things that are bad,

Virtue is loving right; all sin is loving wrong.

We can build any virtue into our thinking by dwelling on that virtue every day.

WINNERS

Bring your best to the moment.

Delight in the success of others as much as you do in your own.

Failing occasionally does not make us failures.

Failure is the condiment that gives success its flavor.

Following God's Word minimizes the success of the secular culture seeking our allegiance.

He who sows sparingly shall reap sparingly; he who sows bountifully shall reap bountifully.

If our expectations are unrealistic, we could end up being consumed by rejection.

If people do their best, no more is required.

If we aren't realistic, our daily plans will always be greater than our actual accomplishments.

Ingredients of a successful life are courage, curiosity, and hard work.

It is not how we start; it is how we finish.

Learn from the mistakes of others; we do not have time to make them all ourselves.

Management is doing things right; leadership is doing the right things.

No one has to win or lose an argument; agree to disagree.

Our approach to understanding should be as though success depended on us.

Our self-concept is our impression of ourselves — we are what we think.

Our self-image determines how we use our time, talent, knowledge, skills, and experiences.

People must accept the cards life deals them, but they must decide how to best play them to win.

Perseverance can overcome pressure.

Perseverance can tip the scales from failure to success.

Quitting is not an option for "believers."

Secret to success: "Do unto others as you would have done unto you."

Sincerity is the greatest secret of personal influence.

Soul-winning (in one's own way) should be the main pursuit of every believer.

Success comes in cans. Failure comes in can'ts.

Success in marriage does not come merely through finding the right mate, but by being the right mate.

Success is having to worry about everything in the world, except money.

Success is leaving the world a better place than we found it.

Success is living every day according to Biblical principles.

Success is often that which we cannot spend (for example, the positive way our children describe us when they are talking with a friend).

The little things people do add up to the big things.

The only place we find success before work is in the dictionary.

The will to win is not nearly as important as the will to prepare to win.

The winner is always part of the answer; the loser is always part of the problem.

There is no success without hardship.

Victory has a thousand fathers, but defeat is an orphan.

We can learn as much from failure as from success.

We cannot "win them all," but we can choose to be a winner rather than a loser.

We win or lose because of the choices we make in life.

When we live purposely, think right, serve generously, and forgive quickly, we lay the groundwork for emotional victory.

Winners accept defeat and get up and go on.

WISDOM

A wise person speaks few words.

Be wisely world, not worldly wise.

It is far easier to be wise for others than to be so for oneself.

Many people wonder if the wisdom of this world has done more good or more harm.

Self-reflection is the school of wisdom.

The next best thing to being wise oneself is to live in a circle of those who are.

The wise see danger ahead and avoid it, but fools keep going and get in trouble.

The wisest individuals are generally those who see themselves as the least so.

Those that know and know that they know are wise. Follow them.

We can tolerate almost any situation when we have hope that things will get better, even when conventional wisdom might suggest we give up.

Wisdom can often arrive in surprisingly quiet ways.

Wisdom should dictate when to speak or not speak and what to say and not say.

Other books by this author include:

The Controversy: Godliness vs. Worldliness
Back to Basics
Words of Wisdom
Words of Wisdom, Too
One Nation Without God
Scripture Servings for Spiritual Strength
Notable Quotables
Matters that Matter, Vol. 1
Matters that Matter, Vol. 2

Books are available from:

www.taddeo.fairwaypress.com
www.csspub.com
www.Amazon.com